Eikonic Leadership is a compendium of biblical insights, real-life experiences, personality assessments, and leadership qualities, skills, and strategies all geared toward knowing who you are as an iconic leader in ministry as well as in the marketplace. This book, inspired by God, coupled by the author's life happenings and her quenchless zeal and passion as a life coach and leadership strategist, should be a go-to book for leaders. *Eikonic Leadership* will take you on a transformational path, navigating the twists and turns of life and the workplace, taking you from usual to unusual, from ordinary to extraordinary, from opaqueness to transparency!

As you read *Eikonic Leadership*, hopefully, it will cause you to do a self-assessment and lead you to recognize that "with every test, with every obstacle, and with every fiery trial," *you* can live and fulfill God's ordained purpose for *your* life! Christ strong!
—Pastor Keith Graham
Now Word Covenant Church
San Antonio, Texas

Iconic—widely known and acknowledged especially for distinctive excellence.

Eight years ago, I had an opportunity to enter a mentor relationship that would forever change the course of my professional and personal development.

When seeking a mentor, you want someone that pushes you out of your comfort zone and challenges you to think outside the box. These were foreign concepts to me in the beginning. While at first this relationship was not always easy, it provided me with the foundation to develop and establish the type of leader I wanted to become.

This book is a must read for men and women alike who recognize they are different from the rest and want to take their leadership abilities to the next level.

Ansonya, you were that mentor who came into my life those years ago, who pushed me out of my comfort zone and helped me become the leader I wanted to be. Thank you for pushing and encouraging me to always reach higher, to stand alone when others wouldn't, and to be the best example of an iconic leader.

—ReShonda Gonzalez

EIKONIC
LEADERSHIP

EIKONIC
LEADERSHIP

8 QUALITIES THAT SEPARATE YOU FROM THE ORDINARY

ANSONYA L. BURKE

EIKONIC LEADERSHIP by Ansonya L. Burke
Published by Principles in Action Consulting, LLC
info@ansonyaburke.com

This book or parts thereof may not be reproduced in any form, stored in a retrieval system, or transmitted in any form by any means—electronic, mechanical, photocopy, recording, or otherwise—without prior written permission of the publisher, except as provided by United States of America copyright law.

Unless otherwise noted, all Scripture quotations are taken from the New King James Version®. Copyright © 1982 by Thomas Nelson. Used by permission. All rights reserved.

Scripture quotations marked NIV are taken from the Holy Bible, New International Version®, NIV®. Copyright © 1973, 1978, 1984, 2011 by Biblica, Inc.™ Used by permission of Zondervan. All rights reserved worldwide. www.zondervan.com. The "NIV" and "New International Version" are trademarks registered in the United States Patent and Trademark Office by Biblica, Inc.™

Scripture quotations marked THE MESSAGE are from *The Message: The Bible in Contemporary English*, copyright © 1993, 1994, 1995, 1996, 2000, 2001, 2002. Used by permission of NavPress Publishing Group.

Copyright © 2019 by Ansonya L. Burke
All rights reserved

Visit the author's website at www.ansonyaburke.com
International Standard Book Number: 978-0-5783001-5-3
E-book ISBN: 978-1-7338730-1-7

While the author has made every effort to provide accurate internet addresses at the time of publication, neither the publisher nor the author assumes any responsibility for errors or for changes that occur after publication. Further, the publisher does not have any control over and does not assume any responsibility for author or third-party websites or their content.

19 20 21 22 23 — 987654321
Printed in the United States of America

CONTENTS

Foreword xvii

Introduction
   You Are Eikonic xix
  Iconic Leaders and the Image of God xxi
  My Coming of Age as an Iconic Leader xxiii
  You Might Be an Iconic Leader If… xxvi
    Misunderstood personality . . . . *xxviii*
    Multiple gifts and talents . . . . *xxviii*
    High standard of excellence . . . . *xxviii*
    Direct . . . . *xxix*
    Individualism—leaders of urgency . . . . *xxix*
    Leader of urgency . . . . *xxx*
  Waiting to Exhale—Breathing in Oxygen,
  Releasing AIR xxx

Chapter 1
  The Eikonic Leader Profile 1
  Advanced in Vision and Focus 4
  Know Who You Are 4
  Break the Mold 5
  The Eight Qualities That Make You, You 6
    1. Idea-centered 7
    2. Passionate 7
    3. Resolute 8

    4. Visionary 9
    5. Disciplined 10
    6. Risk-taking 10
    7. Multidimensional 11
    8. Excellent 11
Whole and Complete 15
Your Oxygen Mask 16

Chapter 2
Nine Spirits That Break the Eikonic Leader— and How to Beat Them 17
Confusion and Depression 17
Deception 18
Jezebel 19
Sanballat and Tobiah 20
Fear 20
Religion 20
Python 21
Bitterness 21
Rejection 22
Temptations or Spiritual Warfare 22
When an Icon Falls 25
Making Room for Imperfection 29
Forgive and Let Go 30
Why Emotional and Spiritual
    Self-Care Is Important 31
Prescription for Releasing Past Hurts 33
    1. Reframe the circumstance 34
    2. Communicate your hurt 35

    3. Forgive them. *36*
    4. Forgive yourself. *37*
    5. Forgive God. *37*
    5. Reestablish trust. *38*
  Your Oxygen Mask 40

Chapter 3
An Unconventional Individual 41
  The Trap of Isolation 42
  Personality Complexities That Contribute
    to Being Misunderstood. 43
  Loner in Love 44
    Difficulty extending trust. *45*
    Challenges with communication and connection *45*
    Unmet expectations *46*
    The marriage of two icons *46*
  Breaking the Saul Mentality 49
  Your Oxygen Mask 52

Chapter 4
Building Your Eikonic Circle of Trust—
Your Tribe 53
  Who Would Jesus Choose? 54
    When it's OK to go alone. *56*
  Five Characteristics of the Ideal Iconic Tribe 57
    1. Your tribe is peculiar. *57*
    2. Your tribe is looking for you. *57*
    3. Your tribe will connect to your voice. *58*
    4. Your tribe seeks transformation. *58*
    5. Your tribe is collaborative. *59*

Attachment Versus Connection. 59
How to Expand Your Tribe 62
   Network 62
   Be open. 62
   Cover new ground. 63
Quality Over Quantity 63
Your Oxygen Mask 65

Chapter 5
Church, Can You Handle Me?. 67
Why Iconic Leaders Are Leaving Ministries. 69
   1. They don't fit in. 69
   2. They are disconnected. 70
   3. They lack support.. 70
   4. They have a ministry unto themselves.. 71
The Right Leader Sees the Iconic Leader
   for Who They Are. 71
The Iconic Leader Needs the Apostolic Leader. 72
An Apostolic Nature 74
   What is the apostolic ministry? 74
   Apostolic tribes 75
When the Church Is Not Your Ministry 77
Don't Despise Divine Alignment 78
Your Oxygen Mask 79

Chapter 6
Anointed but Unannounced. 81
When the Iconic Leader Is Finally Announced 84
Small Is the New Big. 87
Expansion Comes with Pain 88

Chapter 7
Your Secret's Out **91**
   1. Embrace. 93
   2. Affirm 94
      Declare and decree your way out!. 96
   3. Set Boundaries 98
      Setting boundaries for yourself—accountability 99
      Setting boundaries for others—let loyalty decide 100
   4. Care 102
      Take a vacation and enjoy some down time. 103
      If you need help, ask for it. 104
      Say no. 104
      Be proactive in your communication and ask for
        what you need. 105
   Give Yourself AIR 106
   Your Oxygen Mask 106

Chapter 8
Leading the Next Iconic Generation **109**
   Seven Strengths of an Iconic Leader Mentor 110
      1. The iconic leader mentor challenges your thinking. . . 110
      2. The iconic leader mentor is not afraid to upset you. 111
      3. The iconic leader mentor demands excellence. 111
      4. The iconic leader mentor has great character. 112
      5. The iconic leader mentor is a model in
         your area of focus. 112
      6. The iconic leader mentor believes
         in your potential. 112
      7. The iconic leader mentor is a great listener. 113
   Add AIR to Your Mentoring Process 113

How I Give AIR 115
   I know the perfect balance between work and play. ... 116
   I turn correcting mistakes into encouragement and
      valuable lessons. 116
   I address misunderstandings head on. 116
   I don't let anyone get too comfortable. 117
An Iconic Future 117
Your Oxygen Mask 120

Appendix A
The Eikonic Leader Assessment. 121
The Assessment 122
The Results 124
   0–15: The iconic leader in the making 125
   16–30: The ideal iconic leader 125
   31–45: The extreme iconic leader 125
Understanding the Qualities of the Iconic Leader 126
   Individualism—alone in the crowd. 126
   Multiple gifts and talents 127
   High standard of excellence 127
   Misunderstood personality. 128
   Direct personality 128
Now That You Know—What's Next? 129

Appendix B
The Eikonic Leader Soul-Care Assessment 131
The Assessment 133
   Rating scale 134
The Results 141
   0–16: Personal Achievement—Thriving 141

17–32: Depersonalization—*Happy but Exhausted*..... 141
33–48: Burnout—*Emotionally Exhausted }and Unsatisfied*........................ 142

Appendix C
Thirty-One Days of Eikonic Prayers and Declarations.................. 145

Day 1   My Heart's Desire 147
Day 2   I Have Favor............................ 149
Day 3   I Have Influence........................ 151
Day 4   I Am an Heir 153
Day 5   I Am Trustworthy....................... 155
Day 6   I Have the Victory...................... 157
Day 7   I Am Accomplished...................... 159
Day 8   I Have the Mind of Christ 161
Day 9   I Am a Godly Example.................... 163
Day 10 Walk in Love 165
Day 11 I Am Bold and Determined 167
Day 12 I Trust God 169
Day 13 I Am God's Masterpiece 171
Day 14 I Live in Prosperity...................... 173
Day 15 I Take Care of Business 175
Day 16 I Do God's Will......................... 177
Day 17 I Am More Than a Conqueror 179
Day 18 I Prosper in All Things 181
Day 19 I Lead a Blessed Generation 183
Day 20 I Am Accelerated 185
Day 21 I Am Alive in Christ 187
Day 22 I Am Spirit-Led......................... 189

Day 23 I Will not Be Silenced 191
Day 24 I Have a Victor's Mind-set 193
Day 25 I Am Surrounded by the Right People 195
Day 26 I Have More Than I Can Ask 197
Day 27 I Am a Survivor 199
Day 28 God Does Great Things for Me 201
Day 29 I Am Chosen 203
Day 30 I Am Overtaken by Blessings 205
Day 31 I Submit to the Timing of God 207

Notes **209**

Additional Resources **215**

About the Author **217**

FOREWORD

THE HISTORY OF leadership has sought to develop tools that will enable individuals to add to their power and sphere of influence and action while learning to defend themselves against the threats that endanger leaders both personally and academically. *Eikonic Leadership* embodies trust, admiration, and influence, which this book truly exemplifies.

Eikonic Leadership contains materials dealing with the secret places of a leader's heart and answers why leaders often walk alone. Ansonya intrinsically and remarkably applies the basic needs a leader must confront. I believe her goal for *Eikonic Leadership* is to be able to understand governance at the level of their spiritual advancement and apply those concepts with each new level of maturity.

She provides a wide variety of related leadership material to diversify each person's learning experience. She transposes the nurturing of individual productivity and appreciation of quality leadership as crucial components for growth in the areas of ministry, home and family, and employment. Being a leader on the front lines starts with our being positive role models for our children, our spouses, and prospers outwardly.

This book is not only a tool but a primer in understanding

how to live as a leader. It is a heavily researched manual that stirs the heart, mind, and soul of every leader.

Chapter 3 was especially refreshing to read. Ansonya is very transparent that leaders love hard. The context is vital, for not everyone can accomplish authentic influence with the type of heart that is needed to lead a team, carry out the vision, and accomplish a world-wide mission. Great leaders love making people better and unfortunately not everyone wants to commit to themselves.

Eikonic Leadership empowers leaders to divest control as the heart of a leader can often micromanage. This book helps to dispel that.

Enjoy and implement the principles and strategies laced with the oxygenated life-giving thought that Ansonya Burke has released to leaders around the world!

—Pastor Gerald A. Johnson
Gerald A. Johnson Ministries
Faith Culture Church
Round Rock, TX

Introduction

YOU ARE EIKONIC

There's no denying that what led you to pick up this book is the relentless, sometimes nagging feeling you were created to be a big influence in the world. You can feel the greatness that was implanted in you before you were born. It pulses through your veins. The intensity of it wakes you up at night, keeps you working longer and harder than others, and sometimes scares you to death.

Many times we are afraid to claim and say aloud to ourselves and others, "Yes, I was created to make an impact. I am more than others think. I am different. I am not like everyone else. I go hard, and I can't let anything stop me, because I know God called me to an unusual life designed to disrupt the standard."

This is your truth, but you've been trapped by the false idea that this level of confidence means you are not humble. You will be seen as prideful, too much to handle, arrogant, too ambitious, too much of an individual, and untamable. Not only do others see you this way, you have been conditioned to believe this way about yourself too. I've come to challenge you to tear down this false belief if you are to answer the call and live according to the fire burning inside you.

I've come to raise your awareness and challenge you to accept the truth that you are part of an elite group of leaders and influencers who are called to lead the pack, who cannot, for the sake of the kingdom of God, be regular. What am I saying? I am saying this: My friend, you are iconic.

> **Iconic: widely known and acknowledged especially for distinctive excellence.[1]**
> —Merriam-Webster

Now don't get shy with the term. Yes, it is defined as "widely recognized and well-established; widely known and acknowledged especially for distinctive excellence."[2] Yes, it is related to a person who is widely known and usually much talked about. Words such as *ideal, model, genius, archetype, exemplar,* and *paradigm* are often connected with this word, *iconic*. When we use it in our speech, it has a high and lofty connotation. So, within Christian circles, the word can seem to directly contrast what we work hard to tear down, which is anything that will exalt itself against the knowledge of God, and we should do this with expedience.

But let me challenge you here. When it comes time to walk in your unique gifting and assignment on behalf of King Jesus, you need to be confident in who He has created you to be. You must understand there is a level of knowledge and understanding God needs you to align with if you are going to shift the world in His direction. Listen: God has called you to be the type who stirs up and invokes His glory in big ways, over big cultural systems and institutions. This is icon status. This is who you are.

ICONIC LEADERS AND THE IMAGE OF GOD

God desires to see His glory take over every area of our lives and our communities, and He chooses a unique set of individuals who will partner with Him to make this happen. In you, He has put His characteristics of creating something precious out of nothing, a fierce and unshakable love no matter the cost or personal sacrifice, a level of skill and excellence that can't be rivaled, and so much more.

You are an icon—a leader hewn from the Rock of Ages. There's no status quo or normal for you. Your uniqueness and extraordinary abilities empower and excite some but threaten and intimidate others—just as Christ's did. You don't see things the way others do. Your brilliance and supernatural way of viewing the people and circumstances around you are no mistake. This is why you find yourself in conflict with religious spirits and traditional and outdated models which no longer carry the life and energy they once did. This is why you've been rejected, sidelined, and persecuted.

There's another definition for *eikōn* that just about takes my breath away: *eikōn* is an image of heavenly things.[3] This means when you walk in your power that emanates from the glory of God, you display an image of heavenly things on Earth. When you easily spot what's wrong and immediately know the solution, you are displaying heavenly things on Earth. When you are excited about new things and readily embrace change, you display heavenly things on Earth. When you are able to apply unshakable focus and effort to challenging projects and produce masterpiece work, you display heavenly things on Earth. Do you see that? You display the very iconic attributes of God Himself.

I will use the regular spelling—*iconic*—throughout the main body of the book to bring out the principles and revelation God has given me, but do you see why I had to title this book *Eikonic Leadership*? Our English words and definitions rarely do justice to the original intent for a word, especially a word as ancient as *eikon*. This word flowed out of the heart of God at the dawn of creation when He began to build His likeness into Adam:

> For whom he did foreknow, he also did predestinate
> to be conformed to the image of his Son.
> —Romans 8:29, kjv

The word *image* in this verse is the word *eikōn*. Though it's been hard to be you sometimes, God saw you from before time began. He predestined you to be who you are and where you exist at this point in time so you can make a massive impact on the Earth for His glory. Your complexity and the resulting resistance you experience are not accidents. You are iconic for a purpose.

You Are Eikonic

MY COMING OF AGE AS AN ICONIC LEADER

The concept of an iconic leader came to me in a very interesting way. At some point along the way in my church leadership experience, I was called by God as an evangelist and I grew to accept the title. After some high levels of frustration that broke my heart, I vowed to never refer to myself as evangelist again and began to call myself "consultant," "coach," "mentor," and "strategist." Anything, but evangelist.

My hurt was so deep, I did everything I could *not* to teach, *not* to give a word, and sometimes, even *not* to worship. I felt as though I were in a church full of people who didn't see me. Even though I tried everything I knew at the time, I could not connect and felt so alone. I hoped with everything in me to escape this religious, churchy box that didn't quite fit, but in my rebellion, I became more bound. It was a vicious cycle.

All of this, including the many trials in my life with the workplace, children, and home, led me to believe I wasn't good enough to be called by God. The pastors and leaders of churches I attended didn't seem to understand me. Then, others with whom I worked and served, rather than attempting to gain understanding of their own, seemed only interested in following the leaders. In the end, I was left on my own, ostracized.

But my story was not done. Over the years, the Lord, in His grace, brought me to a revelation of who I am in Him. He afforded me divine opportunities to walk through healing and deliverance in many areas concerning the assaults I endured to my identity. Accepting that I am made in His image, I have been strengthened to my core. I am able to confidently be who I am, flaws and all. This was not an easy process, but today, I am proud to say, "I'm more than a life coach. I am an evangelist. I am a minister. I minister. I'm a servant. I love ministry!"

I had so many gifts and talents, I could not harness them into one thing. The leaders around me were ill-equipped to know how to help me flourish, given my many strengths. But God saw and provided a way for me to operate in the fullness of my divine calling and identity. I am forever grateful for His rescue efforts.

Perhaps you struggle with your kingdom assignment like I did. Just remember this one thing: your calling isn't what you do; it's who you are. Don't fight who you are. With the grace and love of God, don't let anyone put you in a box or force you to limit the vastness of what God seeks to accomplish through you. He has a plan for your success. Jeremiah 29:11 says, "For I know the thoughts that I think toward you, says the LORD, thoughts of peace and not of evil, to give you a future and a hope." He knows. Bank on this.

The very things that make it seem like you don't fit are the very things that make you different, unique... *iconic*. As such, you need a church home and a work environment where the leadership is capable of handling your unique gifting. They not only can steward your gift, but they also will cover, cultivate, and promote you because *you* come with the gift.

Operating in an iconic space doesn't mean we are perfect and have everything in place. Many times, we are still figuring things out—especially ourselves. But what we do have is an awareness of the greatness of our God-given purpose and mission, and we live our lives with a passion and determination to see them manifested in the earth.

Many times, however, those who have been anointed and gifted to walk out an iconic assignment hesitate to do so, because of hurt and rejection and several other things that come against our progress.

Initially, this was my issue. It goes without saying that those who walk with any level of anointing and influence pay a price. The Bible is clear that it is through the difficulties in life that what is most precious and valuable is formed. (See James 1:3 and 2 Corinthians 4:8–9.)

I had high expectations for my most intimate relationships with close family and friends. To put it bluntly, they let me down. I am only now scratching the surface of my predestined assignment, having endured great warfare—literally going through it alone—without the benefit of a pastor or leader who fully understood me, and embraced where I was and where I was going.

Because of my "stuff," I struggled. Because of the uniqueness of my gifts and personality, I struggled. Because of the lack of support as I grew into who I was to become, I struggled.

The more I struggled, the more it dawned on me that with every test, with every obstacle, and with every fiery trial, I was growing stronger. What I felt was failure in my life was just part of the fuel I would use to become iconic. What I've come to understand is being perceived as perfect is not a prerequisite for leading others in an iconic way or for presenting them with a greater vision for themselves and their lives than they see on their own.

We all have a specific and unique purpose on Earth. A

destiny scroll exists with our names on it. Some have accidentally stumbled into their destinies while others need a little push to align themselves with what they are called to do.

You Might Be an Iconic Leader If...

Today, the Lord has surrounded me with leaders, mentors, friends, and those I can pour into. I have found my stride and am living in the fullness of who God has called me to be. Out of that, I founded and lead Principles in Action Consulting LLC to support and mentor iconic leaders in the marketplace and Oxygen Global Ministries to equip iconic leaders in the body of Christ. As an iconic leader myself, I am uniquely gifted to influence and impact a group, a nation, or a generation, to move them beyond the status quo and the average; to shift them from dreaming into action, and to empower them to believe the vision is not only possible; it is achievable!

Now it's your turn, iconic leader. I am calling you out from among the masses. Let go of the hurt of being misunderstood and sidelined and step up to the plate. We need you at your best. Take a sober look at who you are—flaws and all—and begin to embrace them. They are yours. We are going to walk through an alignment and restoration process geared toward addressing those deep hurts associated with what doesn't fit or still stings from past offense. God will align and restore you. Trust Him for that and more. He knows who you are (and deep down inside, you do too). Be open to His leading and His voice as He redefines His plans and purpose for you.

As a certified life coach and leadership strategist, I have had the opportunity to engage with numerous individuals in leadership positions. Many easily identify with one or more of the traditional leadership styles:

- Laissez-faire—a hands-off, delegative leadership style often credited with leading to low productivity among teams[4]

- Autocratic—dictator-style leadership in which the leader makes most decisions autonomously. The working environment under this type of leader does not foster creativity or out-of-the-box thinking.[5]

- Participative—also known as democratic leadership, it arises out of collaboration between leaders and the people they guide[6]

There are other leadership types, such as servant, strategic, transformational, transactional, bureaucratic, charismatic, situational, and more. In an effort to keep our conversation relevant, I will stick close to developing an understanding of the type of leader I have been assigned to. If you would like a more rounded study on leadership styles, I recommend *The 5 Levels of Leadership* by John Maxwell, *The 9 Types of Leadership* by Beatrice Chestnut PhD, and *The Road Back to You: An Enneagram Journey to Self-Discovery* by Ian Morgan Cron and Suzanne Stabile.

But know this: you may be among those who do not fit neatly within the mold of any one leadership category. Your leadership dynamic may often be misunderstood and lead to conflict in the workplace, business, and ministry. To others, you don't fit in, but the reality is you don't fit easily into a single leadership box. You fall within a group of extraordinary individuals known as iconic leaders who exhibit multiple styles. Below I share personality traits that may signal whether you are an iconic leader.

Misunderstood personality

Because the iconic leader does not fit into the standard mold, their strong personality is mistaken for arrogance. But the iconic leader is far from being cocky. Does this sound familiar?

Multiple gifts and talents

A jack-of-all-trades and master of *all* may the best way to describe you. There are several layers to who you are. You possess a cornucopia of gifts, making it difficult to place limits on what you can achieve. Yet, you are not pompous about your gifts, preferring to divert attention away from your giftedness.

High standard of excellence

A sure sign you may be an iconic leader is that you have an *extremely* high standard of excellence. This is particularly self-evident in the area of service. For you, excellence does not just describe the desired results when carrying out a task, it is a way of life. The demand for a high standard of excellence coupled with multiple gifts may leave others very uncomfortable.

Direct

Iconic leaders are very direct and to the point. You possess a low tolerance for passive-aggressive behavior. Mind games and long-winded approaches do not find favor with you.

Individualism—leaders of urgency

Iconic leaders may have been taught that it is important to be a team player and that individualism is contrary to productivity. However, if you are an iconic leader, you're OK with the team dynamic, but you'd much rather work with those that have the same sense of urgency. Working with urgency is a combination of thoughts, knowledge, skills, feelings, abilities, and actual behavior. The thoughts and the feelings happen with a gut-level determination that we're going to do something, and the behavior manifests as hyperalertness to what's going on. It's that sense of coming to work every day with a commitment to making something happen. There, the push for excellence isn't misunderstood, intimidating, or out of reach. This sense of urgency transmits in the right way to the right people who will rally around the iconic leader rather than their being put off by it. This is who iconic leaders feel good working with—strong people who understand the iconic leader's direct personality and energy. The iconic leader thrives in groups like this.

However, there are times when the iconic leader feels as if there are not many people who work at this level. In those cases, they may prefer to work alone

Leader of urgency

Procrastination has no room to grow with the iconic leader. If you consider yourself to be a person of urgency and others find it hard to keep up with you, chances are you're an iconic leader. You want things to be done now and will display a high level of impatience when projects or tasks are delayed.

The world is designed so some will lead, and others will follow. Among those who lead, a group of leaders will stand out from the rest, iconic in all they do. If you identify with most of the personality traits I have shared here, then you are an iconic leader. For a more in-depth look at the iconic leader profile, review the Eikonic Leader Assessment in the back of the book and take the test.

My goal in writing this book is to help you arrive at a place where you can embrace your leadership style with confidence and begin to partner effectively with God and others to accomplish the purpose for which you been created.

Waiting to Exhale—
Breathing in Oxygen, Releasing AIR

Consciously or unconsciously, you may be ignoring the warning signs telling you that you may be headed toward a mental, emotional, or spiritual breakdown. These signs may include one or any combination of the following:

- Loss of the vision that God has given you

- Trust issues with people in or adjacent to your inner circle

- Skewed discernment—you are missing signs that things are not right and you end up getting hurt

- Dissociation or isolation—you turn inward and become more silent than usual; though you are in a room full of people, you still feel alone or disconnected

- Depression—no excitement or joy, you've taken to faking and pretending things are OK when they really aren't; nontalkative, closing others out by telling them things are fine, or angry because things are not turning out your way

- Decline of accountability—no longer attending Bible study, prayer life begins to decline, or weary or tired of anything that requires accountability

- Relationship challenges—looking to people for affirmation; misdirecting affection; using people, places, and things to fill the void of wanting closeness; disconnecting from people who really care

- Low self-esteem—no longer feeling like you are called, questioning what God has called you to do

- Uninspired and unmotivated—exhausted and tired all the time, creativity and desire to get up and go have faded, numb to things going on, edgy, experiencing sleeplessness, regretful, little desire to be around people, wishing other's successes were your own

- Dodging—desire to run away from everything

We will explore how to recover and be restored and renewed when life seems to have you beat. We will explore how to pray and ask God for direction, how to identify which friends you can trust and how to decide to whom you should stay accountable. We will look at the benefits of professional counseling and self-care, and so much more.

Leader, this book was designed with you in mind.

If you're like me, your world could be crashing in around you. Your spirit and soul could be gasping for air, yet you still serve and give the same level of excellence as if all were well. But something has begun to die inside—your excitement and drive for your ministry, business, or career, the intimacy in your marriage or other significant relationships, and your own sense of purpose.

God has heard your 911 call. He senses the turbulence in your flight pattern. He knows you need to first take care of you in order for you to really give your best. I'm sure you are familiar with the rule on commercial airlines that says, "Before you assist others, always put your oxygen mask on first." I am going to help you do that. This book is meant to be your oxygen mask.

At the end of each chapter will be "Your Oxygen Mask" exercises to help you pause, breathe, assess, and become more aware of what you need and how you can allow yourself to receive it.

Taking the care to stop and get the oxygen you need to be

You Are Eikonic

your best can be so hard for an iconic leader, but God has set aside special people, places, and resources specially designed to support you in what He has called you to do. But you must first be healed and rejuvenated in your heart and mind so that when help comes, you will recognize the blessing they are and not view them through the disappointments from your past.

It is so important for the iconic leader to come to a place wherein they can trust again. God will resuscitate you as His Spirit breathes into you an extraordinary release, new life, and freedom. You will be nourished and empowered to fulfill God's ordained purpose for your life. God is breathing divine oxygen into you by His Spirit to revive your gifts and calling. You will not be short of breath. Breathing in and out from day to day will no longer be labored.

Once He has restored you, you will be able to breathe AIR in to others. AIR is your call to activate, impart, and release others to fully function as the iconic leaders they are. There's a whole new generation of iconic leaders rising up all around you, and while you are struggling to breathe, they are going around lost like sheep without a shepherd. Just like you need leaders around you who get you and can nurture the unique brand of leader you are, this next generation needs someone too, someone who sees their exception and brilliance. We're going to tackle this later in the book.

So I hope you are ready for an out-of-the-box experience. I hope your exhaustion with ministry, business, and life as usual has you pumped and primed for ministry, business, and life *un*usual. When God found me broken, betrayed, and abandoned, I was more than ready.

It doesn't matter where you are on your journey to growing

into you best self. No matter what it looks like or what the enemy has been trying to say to you, you are on time and you are in the right place to get your life in line for purpose. It doesn't matter if you need a complete spiritual physical, the dreaded annual exam, or a follow-up visit, your arrival to this moment and place is God-ordained. The message of this book called out to you and I am so glad we're here together.

God is calling you out of your rat race and out of an outdated routine whereby you submitted under false loyalty. Those days are over for you. God is ready to apply salve to your open wounds of defeat and breathe new air into your spirit.

Oxygen is needed for endurance and for keeping a fast yet steady pace over a long distance. This what God is bringing in your life. As you apply the anointed ointment of His Word presented in a fresh way, God will manifest Himself in your life and resuscitate your spirit in such a way that you will be able to go the distance. Get ready for a supernatural breath of fresh air. Get ready to receive an overdose of the Holy Ghost. Get ready to be oxygenated in your worship, ministry, marriage, business, and family life. If you are ready to breathe freely again, let's boldly step out together into this process of restoring God's iconic glory in you!

Chapter 1

THE EIKONIC LEADER PROFILE

DO YOU EVER feel like you are in a foreign land? When surrounded by lots of people, do you feel alone, desperately trying to understand why you do not fit in? You may feel alone, but you are not alone in that feeling. I imagine that even within the group in which you feel alone, there are others who feel the same way. I have a theory on why you feel the way you do. If you don't mind, let's take a few steps back in time to when you were a teenager.

As for many others, your teenage years may have been riddled with uncertainty and angst. Attempts to find your place within a community or tribe were without much success. This desperate searching is reminiscent of the 1980s John Hughes's teen flicks such as *Pretty in Pink*, *The Breakfast Club*, *Sixteen Candles*, and *Ferris Bueller's Day Off*. Each movie captures the imagery of how all of us, with intense desire, try to not only make sense of the world and to be able to define our role in it, but also to know we are not alone. These movies help us to see we are not the only ones who think and feel the way we do, neither are we alone in the *way* we do things. This searching is a normal part of our maturation process.

If you've ever watched these icons of pop cinema, you will notice a standard theme: the identification of eclectic teen archetypes. For example, in *The Breakfast Club*, we meet the princess, the brain, the criminal, the jock, and the basket case.[1]

In *Pretty in Pink*, there is a clear line of division between the haves and the have-nots—a class difference—which creates a line that should not be crossed, even for love.[2]

Now, think back to your own high school days. Reflect on where you naturally fit in. If you were like most of those who have become iconic, you didn't naturally fit in anywhere. This is the initial inclination because those who don't fit in normally, usually carry something that those around them will need.

Unlike the teens represented in Hughes's films, you didn't naturally fit in any one group or clique. You were neither one of the popular kids nor were you one of the castoffs. You weren't just a jock, just a nerd, or just a loner. Truth be told, you were probably a little bit of all of the teen archetypes and could more than likely get along with any, or all, of them.

However, if you were to be placed into any specific category, it would most closely resemble the rebel. Because, well, iconic leaders are quite a bit rebellious—not maliciously or intentionally, of course. They just have a way of pushing (or breaking) the boundaries of what is considered acceptable; what society and groups have deemed usual and customary and what is seen as normal, typical, and expected. That you stretch out to see what's possible beyond what everyday people see as possible is what makes you a great visionary and idea-driven leader.

Even today, you never look to be popular or with the

in-crowd, yet everyone seems to know who you are. You do your own thing your own way.

If there is an error, you make the correction.
If there is an issue, you find a solution.
If there is a conflict, you resolve it.
If there is a question, you push for an answer.

You are the one others look to for inspiration, motivation, and confirmation. You always see beyond where things presently stand. You always see another way to do things and get stuff done. You cut to the chase and simplify the complex.

As a teen, you may not have been one of the popular kids, but you were always well known. Everyone knew who you were because you were always involved in the things that made a difference. To this day, people from your high school class know your name; you are trying to figure out who they are. Not because you didn't care to know them, but because, in all honesty, they were more aware of you than you were of them. You had a razor-sharp focus that kept you firmly planted on an upward trajectory, enabling you to accomplish just about everything you set your mind to.

If you stop and think about it, you didn't look to be at the top, at the front of the class, or at the head of the group, but you inevitably found yourself there every time. Others looked for you to be in the lead or to lead them.

You're the unlikely leader—the one who has the passion, resolve, vision, courage to take risks, and the discipline to design a new path independent of societal expectations. You do this not only for yourself, but for others as well!

Advanced in Vision and Focus

Iconic leaders are advanced in vision, having the ability to see past the mediocracy of life while remaining focused on making a difference. Consider, for a moment, Diana Spencer. You don't know who this is? Sure you do. This was the birth name of Diana, Princess of Wales. She was well known, not only for her marriage to Prince Charles, heir to the British throne, but also for her extensive global charity work. She died in a tragic car crash in 1997, but during her life, she was the people's princess. Even individuals who couldn't care less about British monarchy paid much attention to the royal family and deeply celebrated and followed Princess Diana.

It wasn't her celebrity that made her iconic; it was her impact. She influenced so much change on behalf of common people around the world. She captured hearts globally as she ministered to orphans and AIDS victims. She moved those beyond her class. Yet, a friend of Queen Elizabeth II was quoted as saying, "…the pretty girl was a misfit who didn't quite contribute to the things they did and what they wanted her to do in the family."[3] Even Princess Di didn't fit in.

Princess Diana had the ability to impact people, pursue a mission, and embrace a purpose beyond herself. These things made her an iconic leader.

Know Who You Are

One day the same will be said about you. There is a saying that cemeteries are the wealthiest places on Earth. It is there the unique treasures of humanity are buried—along with dreams, unfulfilled desires, and thwarted destinies. Many would-be iconic leaders died without leaving an impact on the world simply because they did not know who they were. The scriptures say we perish where knowledge is lacking (Hosea 4:6). Ignorance of who we are can stunt creativity, passion, and legacy.

True appreciation may not always be shown to every iconic leader in life, but if it is not, the realization will set in after they have passed from this life, their impact greater than anyone realized. Their names and the very essence of who they were will not be forgotten.

Being iconic is more than doing great things. It is more about being than doing. Knowing who you are in Christ and what gifts He has given you to be a blessing wherever you are planted is the essence of being iconic. You are iconic. Everything you are and do flows from the eight qualities we'll describe over the net few pages.

Remember, we are human beings, not human doings. When we try to validate our existence by what we do, we sometimes miss this simple reality: we already are.

Break the Mold

We all want to fit in and to have a sense we belong. There is nothing wrong with this desire. However, as an iconic leader, if you don't recognize where and how you fit into the whole, you will find yourself and your unique set of gifts and divinely assigned purpose continuously diminished and depressed. Yes, you may have had difficulty fitting in the past, but my belief is that this came as a result of your lack of knowing who you truly are. We have a harder time feeling that we fit when we can't really see ourselves the way God does. We may feel as if we need to be who others want us to be and become frustrated when it doesn't feel authentic.

There is a place for the iconic leader—a place ordained by God for you to build and expand both yourself and those with whom you work. It is a place where you will not feel as if you have to resign yourself to fitting into any preconceived mold. You were not made for that. You must know who you are and fully operate as you were designed, and this book will help you discover this. If you don't, you will find yourself either squeezing into a life not meant for you or assigned to roles that others determine best suit you and their agendas. You won't have the impact or influence for which you were purposefully created. You were made to break the mold.

The Eight Qualities That Make You, You

One of the most important things for an iconic leader to know and be confident in is who they are. In my experience as an iconic leader and mentor to leaders of this type, I have come to know we all have in common these eight characteristics: idea-centered, passionate, resolute, visionary and prophetic, discipline, risk-taking, multidimensional, and excellence. Let's take a closer look at these eight qualities that simultaneously set you apart and make you an asset, drawing people to you.

1. Idea-centered

Iconic leaders love ideas and generate high volumes of effective ones, doing so in their sleep, so to speak. If you are familiar with *StrengthFinders 2.0*, you are familiar with one of the traits it has popularized. It's called ideation. Iconic leaders are ideators.

Ideate essentially means "to see." This skill or strength is connected to "creativity, experimentation, and dreaming," without which businesses, organizations, and people would be far less innovative and profitable. They would stagnate and become outdated. They thrive when given the opportunity to generate original ideas. Often labeled deep thinkers or over-thinkers, iconic leaders lead and influence others because of their ideas, not because of relationship skills. Examples of ideation at work can be seen in leaders like Steve Jobs, who grew Apple into tech behemoth it is today, or in activists like Martin Luther King Jr., whose ideas helped to bring equality and civil rights to people in the US and around the world.

The iconic leader is energized by change and fascinated by ideas. They revel in seeing things "from a strange but strangely enlightening angle."[4] They opt to work independently instead of with groups. They are unusual and are often frustrated with the mundane, especially when there are better ways to do things, yet no one is "willing to consider the changes you suggest."[5]

2. Passionate

Passion is an "intense desire or enthusiasm for something."[6] Other words for passion are *fervor*, *zeal*, and *ardor*. Iconic leaders feel deeply about issues, concerns, or missions to which they are uniquely called. The reasons behind their passion may be simple or multifaceted.

Passion, without a doubt, is a driving force that motivates them. In fact, authentic and genuine passion for others and the intense desire to witness their transformation into someone greater than they previously imagined or hoped for serves as a catalyst that builds momentum in this engaging and empowering leader.

Passion is an offspring of desire. There can be no transformative process or manifestation outside of what we desire. An iconic leader must always have an answer to the question, "What do I want?" Our passion connects us to the answer, the catalyst upon which success can be built. It is God who said, "I will give you the desires of your heart" (Ps. 37:4). The iconic leader depends on God to do just that.

3. Resolute

Armed with a firm determination to do all they think or imagine, iconic leaders are resolute. Once they set their hearts and minds on a course of action, their sights become fixed on seeing it through. The Word of God tells us that as His children, we are to be "steadfast, immovable, and always abounding in the work of the Lord." (1 Cor. 15:58). This spirit of resoluteness is not optional for iconic leaders. There is an innate assurance, a high level of confidence within, which secures them. They have a certainty and keen awareness of why they are and what they are purposed, gifted, and anointed to do.

Even if an iconic leader encounters momentary internal conflict based on external opposition or a personal issue, they move not only to commiserate and discuss a plan of action but to actually act in spite of it all.

With this resolve, they are not easily swayed by discouragement, and while they are not invincible, iconic leaders are rarely shaken off course by external influences.

4. Visionary

Vision is the ability to see or perceive beyond that which is obvious to the natural eye. Merriam-Webster's online dictionary defines *vision* as "a manifestation to the senses of something immaterial" and also "unusual discernment or foresight." *Perception, intuition, conceiving,* and *seeing* are synonyms of this word.[7]

Vision is the type of sight that allows an engineer to see beyond the forest of trees into a community of family homes. It is the inspiration that supports a tribe or group in being able to see something new that will enrich and improve their current situation, circumstance, or comprehension. It is the capacity to see, with vividness, a tomorrow better than today, and helping everyone involved to move toward a shared view for the future.

The iconic leader must be able to meet their network right where they are in today's reality yet communicate a greater future state well enough that their followers engage and contribute to the manifestation of that vision.

"With no vision, people perish" (Prov. 29:18). This Scripture tenet implies, from my perspective, that where leadership is lacking in vision, there is sure to be chaos and death of innovation, ideas, and implementation. We cannot move forward without them.

5. Disciplined

The fifth characteristic of all iconic leaders is discipline: the ability to demonstrate a high-level focus in order to keep moving forward and carry out their plans. Discipline manifests as self-mastery and focus. It is about being able to "train oneself to do something in a controlled and habitual way";[8] "the rigor or training effect of experience, adversity, etc."[9]

Difficulties will come. Opposition will come. Distractions will come. However, iconic leaders are capable of maintaining consistent momentum in the face of it all. They will not, nor can be, deterred from their path.

Many times, one's level of discipline is the deciding factor between being simply a good leader and becoming an iconic one. There is no room for wishy-washy, constantly wavering, or some-timey leadership. When others leave or are absent, iconic leaders show up!

6. Risk-taking

A sixth characteristic innate to iconic leaders is risk-taking, defined as the ability to move forward irrespective of any potential danger or prevailing consensus that opposes their assignment or path. Risk-taking is "the act or activity in which someone takes risks in order to achieve a goal or obtain a benefit."[10] Courage, boldness, fortitude, and audacity are complementary traits that make risk-taking an attribute of this leadership type.

This risk-taking capability extends itself without regard to personal detriment because the end goal or outcome is greater than one's self. Beyond being creative, visionary, and innovative, risk-takers go beyond the norm, the common, and the everyday. They don't just think outside the box; they operate as if there is no box!

As risk-takers, iconic leaders are trailblazers, much like Captain James Tiberius Kirk. "They boldly go where no one has gone before!"

7. Multidimensional

Blessed with above-average gifting in multiple areas, the iconic leader often has a hard time narrowing down their focus. They master everything they put their hands to and will not be boxed in.

8. Excellent

I'm often amazed at those who present raggedy things in the marketplace and in ministry and then expect others to flock to them. If God gave you a ministry or kingdom mission, surely He also gave you the requisite resources to present it with excellence.

Excellence is a word used in many corporate, church, and mentoring arenas. It is defined as "the quality of being outstanding or extremely good" and is synonymous with *greatness, caliber, eminence, skill, talent, distinction,* and *mastery*.[11]

For entrepreneurs, part of being excellent is having a strong brand identity. For those in ministry, it's ensuring you have the right people in place to help build the vision God gave you. In mentorship, it's making sure you have someone who understands the importance of interacting with you in a disciplined manner to coach you to excellence. The overarching point with regard to excellence being that, whether you are an entrepreneur, visionary, or pastor, operating with a quality of excellence is essential to producing an excellent result.

It is easy for someone to say they value the quality of excellence, yet much more difficult to demonstrate it. When you are not operating with excellence, all you do only amounts to mediocrity.

This is not an issue for the iconic leader. Take Barack Obama. We really don't even need to say *what* he was, as his last name alone is sufficient to identify him both nationally and internationally. Aside from the title he held for two presidential terms, his character is what will be remembered most by the majority. Inaugurated the forty-fourth president of the United States and recipient of the 2009 Nobel Peace Prize, this black man came on the scene at a time when the country was in the throes of near depression, thought to have been caused, in part, by the preceding administration. His rallying cry of "yes, we can" broke down barriers, galvanized an entire nation, and gave people hope. But he didn't just say the words; he backed them up with action, so much so that when he gave his farewell address on January 10, 2017, he added the words, "Yes, we did."

Nothing Obama did could be interpreted as mediocre. Everything he did, he did to serve the people, and in spite of the opposition he faced on a daily basis, he endeavored to motivate each citizen to believe in their own capacity to bring about change.

> *Mediocre* in Latin means "halfway to the top [of a rugged mountain]."[12] Webster's defines it as "of only moderate quality; not very good, so-so, average, middle of the road, lackluster, fair-to-middling."[13]

Iconic leaders have an extremely high standard of excellence, especially in the areas of service. They innately move in excellence, exemplifying it in three primary ways: how they think, the words they speak, and the way they act.

Iconic leaders think

Iconic leaders know that before they can begin a project, start a mission, or build toward an ideal, cause, or vision, they must first give thought to the relevant costs and details required to bring it to manifestation. They do not do things on a whim, because they know that doing so would invite disaster, or ultimately, failure.

Iconic leaders speak

Iconic leaders speak words of life, power, purpose, and provision in such a way that the hearer is motivated, strengthened, and moved to action.

Iconic leaders act

Iconic leaders realize excellence is most often recognized in its finished form: the polish, the perfect performance, the victory. But true, godly excellence, lies in the details, and it is demonstrated via each extra effort, each practice, and each time you give 100 percent, even when no one is watching. You build your excellence brick by brick and good decision after good decision.

In this area, the prophet Daniel exemplifies a person of excellent spirit, even in the midst of adverse conditions. His character is defined in great detail in the Book of Daniel. Insomuch that the words used to describe him are that in everything he did, he did so in excellence (Daniel 6:3). His excellence was evident not just in the tasks before him, but also in the spirit in which he performed those tasks. Remember, Daniel was a part of the remnant of Jews who were in captivity in Babylon under King Belshazzar, son of King Nebuchadnezzar. This time was significant because among the many lessons we can glean from Daniel, we see that, although circumstances may not always be ideal, we do not have to compromise our character in reaction to those circumstances.

> Inasmuch as an excellent spirit, knowledge, understanding, interpreting dreams, solving riddles, and explaining enigmas were found in this Daniel, whom the king named Belteshazzar, now let Daniel be called, and he will give the interpretation.
> —Daniel 5:12

A study of Daniel also demonstrates that although there may be those among us with similar gifts and talents, often one seems to shine brighter or be more effective. Although the king called others with the same gift, none were as effective as Daniel.

I personally hold myself to a high standard of excellence. I made a vow that I would do my best to operate in the spirit of excellence in everything I do. I really enjoy five-star hotels, fine dining (for the quality and service), and retreats (for the environment and sense of community).

People can tell how you value not only yourself but also how you value them by the effort you put into what you do. How you carry yourself speaks louder than your words ever will. Be committed to the task at hand, to do it with excellence or not at all. Doing things for the kingdom in a mediocre way diminishes what God is due. He is an excellent God who has given us His excellent Son. Therefore, how could you offer Him anything less than excellence?

WHOLE AND COMPLETE

Certainly, one or all of these characteristics may be attributed to individuals who play a role in influencing others. This list does not exhaust all of the inherent characteristics in the iconic leader profile. Nevertheless, an iconic leader will indeed possess and exhibit at least these eight attributes.

The iconic leader must embody all of these traits in order to be successful. When they do not, the desired results are not achieved. For example, if a leader is passionate, resolved, visionary, and willing to take risks but doesn't remain disciplined, engaged, and active all the way to the end of the matter, their followers will become confused, deflated, and uninspired. The same holds true if certain other characteristics are embodied yet not displayed alongside others in the heart of the icon. The dream dies with them.

It is critical to note it is not important the iconic individual be a famous person or hold a lofty title or position. As we've mentioned previously, persons who share these characteristics can be found in many different arenas and within various circles. The key to their being iconic lies in their leaving a legacy beyond their lifetimes—what they say, stand for, and create will remain relevant and be remembered for generations.

In the coming chapters, we will look at several other factors unique to the iconic leader profile—the spiritual enemies that come to sabotage their mission, how iconic leaders are judged and misunderstood because of their unconventional approach, the difficulties iconic leaders face in relationships, the challenges they face within the four walls of the church, and more.

Your Oxygen Mask

1. Think back over your youth. When was the first time you recognized you were different than others? What were the circumstances? How did your life change from that point on?

2. As you read the eight qualities of an iconic leader, with which ones did you connect the most? Why? Which ones are you hesitant to own? What makes you want to separate yourself from those qualities?

3. How do you feel about the directive to know yourself? Do you know yourself well? Name some things you can do to better know yourself and what you are capable of.

Chapter 2

NINE SPIRITS THAT BREAK THE EIKONIC LEADER— AND HOW TO BEAT THEM

THE DYNAMIC YET rare makeup of the iconic leader makes them a threat to the kingdom of darkness. There are nine spiritual weapons the enemy forms against you, but God has given you even greater weapons to overcome them. These nine spirits are confusion and depression, deception, Jezebel, Sanballat and Tobiah, fear, the spirit of religion, python, bitterness, and rejection. Let's take a look now.

CONFUSION AND DEPRESSION

The enemy knows if you are aligned correctly, you will walk in authority and purpose. Therefore, his focus is to get you to doubt and mistrust. As the enemy launches his fiery darts at you, his goal is to get you to begin doubting whether you were even called to ministry or to the assignment that has been given to you. Leaders who fall to his tactics question, "Is this where I am supposed to be? Is this really my purpose?"

You know when this spirit is attacking because you won't

want to pray or go to church. You begin to stop trusting your inner self. You feel like your discernment is off.

To fend off the tag-teaming spirits of confusion and depression, pick up the Word of God, that you may fight with the sword of the Spirit. I remember when I was going through such a time in my life and I just could not pray. I picked up my copy of *Prayers that Avail Much* by Germaine Copeland. In the book, I found the prayers that matched the situations I was in and used those prayers as weapons against the enemy. At that time, I didn't have it within myself to pray, so I prayed those prayers written by someone else to make sure I fed something spiritual into my system. At this time, you also need your tribe. You do not want to go through something like this alone.

Deception

Unity and authenticity within the tribe is important for the work to be fruitful. However, this spirit of deception will plant those among you who talk the language of the tribe yet are only in the group for self-gain. They are not true community partners. They are out to get what they can from you and others in the tribe. They are there to steal, kill, and destroy the dream and purpose God has ordained for you. In this type of attack, people will use the Word of God for self-gain. They will use truth wrapped in a lie and try to apply Scripture to back it up. This spirit also presents itself in the form of someone who is full of self-promotion and does not give God any glory. Everything they do is for self-gain. (See 1 Timothy 4:1.)

JEZEBEL

This spirit's mission is to assassinate your character and attack your relationships. It is a controlling spirit that causes people to whisper, stir up gossip, and incite hatred, opening the door for others to believe lies against you. Its aim is to destroy your credibility and keep others from connecting with you. The very nature of this spirit, its personality and the way it operates, makes it very dangerous once it sets up shop within a leader.

The Jezebel spirit controls, manipulates, and dominates more in male authorities—husbands, pastors, leaders, spiritual parents, and the like. Multiple pastors and leaders have aborted their assignments because of this spirit.

This spirit actually seeks out people whose trust it can easily gain. Then it begins to do its damage. Before you know it, it is in your space. It has influenced your best friend, caused coworkers to question you, and wreaked havoc in your home life. This spirit is very subtle and subjugating.

You can avoid being influenced by this spirit by having people to whom you are accountable, people who know you very well and who will recognize when you begin doing things that are out of order. Stay humble and connected to the heart of God; doing so will also be to your great advantage, so conviction will arise in your life when this spirit knocks at your door. (See Revelation 2:20.)

Sanballat and Tobiah

Sanballat and Tobiah are the enemies that bring strong opposition to your influence and what God is trying to accomplish through you. These spirits assassinate your character and bring false accusations against the work of people in your tribe who are helping you accomplish your purpose. These spirits release attacks against your influence to stop your momentum. They work to discourage you from building the God-given vision.

This spirit camouflages itself in sheep's clothing, which looks, for example, like someone who says God has assigned them to you and who offers to come to work with you. Now someone like this could truly be a God-send. On the other hand, when this someone sabotages you and tears you down such that you do *not* fulfill your purpose or your passion, they are not there to assist you. They are there to oppose and to stop your influence. (See Nehemiah 4:1–8.)

Fear

Without faith, it is impossible to please God (Heb. 11:6), so the spirit of fear has as its function getting you to operate in unbelief. It will pressure you to doubt what God has told you and doubt that the promise will come to pass, to operate from a place of fear rather than power and strength in God.

Religion

The religious spirit, or spirit of routine, will stifle the fire within you and get you wrapped up in the normality of things, causing you to forget to maintain the critical intimacy of your relationship with God. You must honor the ministry, title, name, or platform because you worship and have a relationship with God, but do not let the traditions and rituals of man cause the Word of God to become mundane and ineffective in your life, leading you to have a form of godliness devoid of any real power (2 Tim. 3:5).

Python

Author Jennifer LeClaire says, "One of the only named spirits in the Bible, the python spirit is a coiling spirit that works to squeeze out the breath of life (the Holy Spirit) and cut off your lifeline to God (prayer)."[1] References to this spirit can be found in Acts 16:16.

In the natural, a python literally squeezes the life out of its prey. In the spiritual realm, Satan does the exact same thing, coiling tighter and tighter around our spiritual lives until we are suffocated in the spirit, defeated and closing in on spiritual death, or extinction. As soon as you feel the grip loosen and believe you might be able to come up for air, the python spirit squeezes again, bringing on another trial. There seems to be no way to escape the continuing string of defeats.

Bitterness

Bitterness that takes root in the iconic leader's heart can manifest as unforgiveness, resentment, and grudges. Bitterness may display itself when it seems certain leaders constantly send subtle messages from the pulpit. In other cases, they covertly ostracize those by whom they have been offended, greeting them in public, but then talking against them to other leaders within the church and not allowing those leaders to form their own opinions. If not dealt with, bitterness can metastasize or spread like a cancer in the workplace or ministry. Bitterness will cause one to attack people rather than problems. (See Hebrews 12:15.)

Rejection

Rejection, resulting from being misunderstood, often hinders the iconic leader. Betrayal, a close relative of rejection, happens when people who you believe love you start acting like they don't know or understand you. This can lead to disappointment and inability to trust. Some of the symptoms of rejection are loneliness, isolation, and alienation. This spirit can lead a person to be critical of others and exhibit other negative behaviors to compensate for feeling as they do. A rejected leader may have a hard time loving and believing others when they provide compliments or positive feedback. Self-doubt often follows, making it hard for the suffering leader to move forward in confidence and self-assurance. (See Matthew 13:54–58.)

Temptations or Spiritual Warfare

You'd think being in church leadership would ensure you're not tempted to fall into the same temptations as, say, leaders in the marketplace. But that is not the case. Jesus assures us even we who are in the household of faith will encounter trouble in the world (John 16:33) and in the body of Christ. The Apostle Paul addressed the early church on many issues involving interpersonal issues among believers—contention, gossip, arguing, lying, deception, and more. (See 2 Corinthians 12:20 for one example.)

In Leviticus 19:16, God tells His people not to spread slander or gossip among themselves. All of the spirits mentioned above are about character assassination and aborting the mission. To *assassinate* means "to murder (a usually prominent person) by sudden or secret attack often for political reasons" and "to injure or destroy unexpectedly and treacherously."[2] Character assassination is about killing a man's character, killing him, metaphorically, by the things for which he is known in his corner of the world.

These nine spirits are harmful to you and your ministry. It is, therefore, imperative you are aware of the signs associated with these spirits and take hold of the Word to combat them. In addition to staying in the Word of God, keep your tribe and accountability partners close.

I and many of the iconic leaders I mentor have been attacked by these spirits. During the time my name and reputation were slandered, I wanted to really tell the world, "I am not guilty. They are lying." I had to remain quiet and allow the Lord to fight my battles. It was a horrible experience, but experiences like that reveal who is truly with you and who is against you. People I thought were with me, covenant friends, fell by the wayside, unable to withstand the pressure.

When you have an assignment on your life—something you are called to do that's bigger then you—expect a tsunami of temptations and attacks to show up in full force. Know the enemy will try to abort your assignment. Arm yourself with the breastplate of righteousness and all the things Ephesians 6:10–20 brings. Lean in to your tribe and let them know what's taking place. Ask them to pray and hold you accountable. Don't hide and try to deal with these attacks by yourself. When you do, the enemy pours it on thick because he attacks most when he perceives you as weak. In this assaulted state, you will feel greater effect from his attempts to intimidate and manipulate you.

The nine spirits we explored above can manifest themselves as both temptations aimed at getting iconic leaders to take on the characteristics of these spirits or manifest in others and come at the iconic leader like spiritual attacks. In either case, you need to be ready to wage spiritual warfare to protect the unique gifts, anointing, and assignments you have as an iconic leader.

Being self-aware is such a good gift to have when dealing with the above types of attack. When you know yourself and what symptoms to look for, you are able to run to your accountability leaders at the first sign of trouble to ensure you don't fall into the pitfalls the enemy has set to trap you. (See Matthew 5:11–12.)

We will explore how to build an inner circle of trust—that is, your tribe—in a later chapter. Knowing how to construct that all important group is an important part of properly managing your unique set of gifts.

Nine Spirits That Break the Eikonic Leader and How to Beat Them

WHEN AN ICON FALLS

Every leadership model, test, training, and so on claims to have all the answers to the manifold challenges of leadership. Each perspective emphasizes certain qualities, and, in the absence of clear direction, we search desperately for answers. But the truth is, there is no simple leadership formula which meets every need we have in ministry, the marketplace, or life mentorship experiences. What I am sharing in this book is what God has given me through wisdom, experience, and education as it pertains to the iconic leader and is what I have seen bring them to the strength and confidence they need to shine. Yet without resources like this and without leaders with eyes to see who we really are, many of us stumble and fall. We are met with immense negative perceptions. We are greatly misunderstood, not only by others, but even within ourselves. And we are not properly equipped to handle the onslaught of demonic attack. How do we deal with the laundry list of challenges we inevitably will face without giving up and rejecting our divinely assigned role?

To provide a starting point for this discussion, let's go back to 2010. During this time, mainstream media began reporting that the late Bishop Eddie Long, then senior pastor of New Birth Missionary Baptist Church, had been accused of sexual coercion by four underage male members of his congregation. Until this time, Bishop Long was viewed as an icon of strong spiritual leadership, not only for those in his parish but also by other leaders and clergy, nationally and internationally. His preaching ministered to the lives of many and the church he had pastored since 1987 grew from a membership of three hundred to over twenty-five thousand during those thirty years under his leadership.[3]

Among both controversial and celebrated events throughout his pastoral leadership, in 2006, Bishop Long was selected by the family of Martin Luther King Jr. to host and officiate the funeral services for Mrs. Coretta Scott King, the late civil rights leader's widow. In attendance were three living former presidents—George H. W. Bush, Bill Clinton, and Jimmy Carter—and then sitting president, George W. Bush.

At the conclusion of the matter, the young men received an undisclosed settlement. Despite the controversy, upon Bishop Long's death, many mourned the loss of this man who had left a legacy of writing, teaching, and preaching the Word of God.

Through this example we understand that no matter how successful a leader may be in one or more areas of life, due to human failings, some may struggle with external or internal challenges, sometimes privately and sometimes publicly.

Speaking of Dr. King, a 1968 *Time* Magazine profile of him shared that he twice attempted suicide in his early teens, following the death of his grandmother.[4] Into adulthood, King continually suffered with seasons of severe depression, yet refused treatment; stating the following to a conference of psychologists in 1967:

> There are some things concerning which we must always be maladjusted if we are to be people of good will.[5]
>
> —Dr. Martin Luther King Jr.

To put it another way, it's as if the thing that causes a leader to limp is the exact thing that helps them to have empathy or compassion for others; the reminder of their own pain is what keeps them mindful of other people's need to receive grace in their areas of weakness. The Apostle Paul refers to this imperfection in one's person as "a thorn in the flesh." (See 2 Corinthians 12:7–9.) He wrote about his personal thorn, without specifying exactly what the thorn is or whether it is actually physical in nature. There are varying theories as it relates to this, however, there seems to be general consensus as to the purpose of the thorn in his life.

The thorn represents a flaw or imperfection. This is critical, because it disproves the idea that perfection is a prerequisite for iconic leadership. In fact, the apostle uses his flaw as a focus or aid in his teaching and mentoring. Paul affirms the necessity of the thorn in that he says it evokes a sense of humility. He recognizes the potential threat of being controlled or influenced by the spirit of prideful conceit stemming from his ability to use certain unique gifts given directly to him by God. The thorn is a constant source of pain, but it is also a continual reminder that although he is highly gifted, educated, and admired, he is also flawed…and he needs God.

Therefore, whether the challenges an iconic leader must deal with are external or internal, physical or mental, spiritual or emotional, support lies in the realization that all leaders, good, great, and even iconic, are human, made of flesh, and, inherent in that flesh is a varied combination of gifts and frailty. First Peter 1:24 says, "All flesh is as grass, and all the glory of man as the flower of the grass. The grass withers, and its flower falls away."

Knowing this, the key to success for an iconic leader is not in being so concerned with how to deal with each of the myriad of "thorns," allowing them to become obstacles to manifestation. But instead, as Dr. King and the Apostle Paul so eloquently demonstrate, allowing the thorn or limp to become a catalyst continually fuels your humanity.

The reality then is an iconic leader may not walk in perfection nor should it be expected they do. It can be challenging to see a leader in such light. There is a story told among Christian mystics that being privy to the most intimate places of God and noticing His apparent weakness for humanity such that He would conceive of a plan to save all humanity by becoming human is what led to Satan's fall.

The culture of the pulpit has caused many to esteem themselves as walking in perfection. One might not think a miracle worker can get sick or one who preaches prosperity might fall prey to poverty. Such events seem contradictory and may cause one who lashes out against sin to themselves fall victim to it. Yet, the reality of leadership is there are moments of being up, yet the law of nature states that what goes up will also come down. Leaders rise. Leaders fall.

Scriptures cite men like Elijah, whose effectual and fervent prayer life produced great results, as men of like passions, just like us. Even Jesus is referred to as one who knows the things we struggle with (Isa. 53:3).

Iconic leaders are special by what drives them, but their above average qualities do not make them immune to a fall. They are not defined by how many times they fall nor the nature of their mistakes, but how they respond to it.

MAKING ROOM FOR IMPERFECTION

Iconic leaders tend to hold themselves to a higher standard due to their own expectations and are generally harder on themselves than on others. This not unique to those who operate at this level of leadership. Still, the perception of those who are watching is that if these leaders are sitting in that position or hold that title, they must have it all together.

It is imperative that you are not afraid to make an error or exhibit transparency. You are not perfect nor are you called to be. Above all, don't make the mistake of buying into and believing your own press release. The truth is one can be flawed and iconic at the same time. Being flawed does not equate to being a failure. Submit your failings to God and, in the words of the Apostle Paul, "…count not myself to have apprehended: but this one thing I do, forgetting those things which are behind, and reaching forth unto those things which are before, I press toward the mark for the prize of the high calling of God in Christ Jesus" (Phil. 3:13–14).

Paul uses a strong word in this context: *forget*. It is the same sentiment God uses in relation to our sins: "I will remember them no more." When God says this, His words imply a reset so divinely acute, the very act in question is absolutely erased from creation's database. It's as if it never happened.

Remember, you can be imperfect and still have impact!

Forgive and Let Go

As we come to the end of this chapter, I want to address the very necessary principle of forgiveness and letting go, first as a godly directive, but also as one of the most important aspects of an iconic leader's self-care and spiritual warfare protocol. As I began to think about how I wanted to address this, I remembered a news story I read not too long ago.

On August 25, 2018, the *Christian Post* reported that Pastor Andrew Stoecklein of Inland Hills Church (Chino, CA) was pronounced dead after attempting to take his own life inside his church.[6] As I read this news, my heart broke for his wife and three children, as well as for his church family and community. Depression is real, and pastors are not exempt from it, neither are they defective because they experience it. As I have been in position to counsel pastors and leaders at this level, I have seen similar signs among iconic leaders. Many leaders would share their struggles with depression, insecurity, inadequacy, and anxiety, but may feel that sharing these details would make them seem weak, self-serving, or even spiritually undeserving of the post in which they serve.

When it comes to releasing hurts, I recommend we learn to watch for our own signs of being overwhelmed and emotionally distressed. In this generation, we expect so much of ourselves and our leaders. We want to be business savvy, Instagram-quotable celebrities, fully accessible, deeply spiritual, not too young or too old, and so much more. If we don't quite measure up to someone's expectation at any given moment, our ministry or business is given a two-out-of-five-star rating on Google. Wow! We have reduced the ministry to Google star ratings!

As we move forward into this brief exploration of your heart and soul, let me recommend that you pray for your pastor or leader and support your church faithfully. I know you may have issues with the organization, but you must remain in a place of humility and grace. No one knows all any leader endures, and when any of us are in a position where we are not at our best, we each hope to receive grace.

Why Emotional and Spiritual Self-Care Is Important

In his article "Five Reasons Pastors Get Depressed (and Why They Don't Talk About It)," Thom Rainer points out "too many pastors have been taught that depression is a sign of failure in ministry, that it is something that must be hidden from view. Those are lies, blatant lies. Please get help. Now."[7] He goes on to list these five reason pastors remain silent about their struggles:

1. Spiritual warfare—the enemy is intent on destroying their ministry

2. The surprising reality of pastoral leadership—they didn't know the full scope of what they were in for

3. Sense of inadequacy—feels like everything that went wrong is their fault

4. Critics and bullies—the constant and steady stream of criticism wears on them

5. Loneliness—it's hard to find true friends

It is not difficult to see how these kinds of feelings creep into the mind and heart of the high-performing iconic leader. This is why spiritual deliverance and emotional healing are important and must be ongoing.

Hanging on to bitterness, betrayal, unforgiveness, and anger are essentially death traps strategically placed by the enemy to thwart the forward movement of your divine assignment. However, God has given us every access to the host of heaven and all of its weapons to stomp on the enemy and maintain our position. Finding your tribe, as we previously discussed, is another way to safeguard yourself against isolation, Satan's favorite place for you to be as he wages war against you.

Keep this in mind as we look at how you have responded to people's treatment of you because of your difference. Consider that you are not simply fighting against people and what they can do, but you are fighting unseen powers and dark forces with a much more insidious and final plan to end the effectiveness of your life's work and leadership. Consider also it is God who fights for you and your victory is secure in Jesus. I also recommend you take the Eikonic Leader Soul-Care Assessment I've prepared for you in appendix B. This is especially for when you are feeling uninspired and unmotivated for longer than you are used to. We need what you have inside of you to remain active and engaged. You are so important to what God is doing.

Prescription for Releasing Past Hurts

Sometimes our hurts, disappointments, let downs, and betrayals feel so painful we lose sight of our true responsibility as a leader when it comes to our response to these offenses. We must respond in a way that actually moves us forward toward what God has called us to do. Forgiveness and letting go are not actions we take only when we feel good enough to do them, but they are conditional mandates from God. If we don't extend forgiveness, God will not forgive us.

Matthew 6:14–15 says,

> For if you forgive men their trespasses, your heavenly Father will also forgive you. But if you do not forgive men their trespasses, neither will your Father forgive your trespasses.

If we do not let go of the past, bitterness will set in and we will become hard, bitter, prideful, and impenetrable to the still, small voice of the Holy Spirit. When this happens, we cannot hear Him as He attempts to ready us to press on to higher things.

The apostle Paul shared how he took hold of this principle in his life when he said, "Forgetting those things which are behind and reaching forward to those things which are ahead, I press toward the goal for the prize of the upward call of God in Christ Jesus" (Phil. 3:13–14). Unforgiveness stagnates the iconic leader, so you must be ready always to forgive and release any offenses to God. He says vengeance is His; He will repay (Rom. 12:19). Can you take Him at His Word and trust Him to deal justly with those who hurt you?

If so, I want to introduce you to a simple prescription for unforgiveness I believe will enable you to function at your best and sustain a high level of authentic and passionate engagement with the people and assignments specific to you.

1. Reframe the circumstance.

It may be hard to believe, but some hurts come with a hidden blessing. One of the things I have learned across my years in ministry and leadership is we do not arrive at any significant place of promotion without experiencing some kind of betrayal. Bear with me on this. I do not intend to speak negatively over your life or future endeavors, but think about this:

a. You are moving to a new level.

Daniel was betrayed. Joseph was betrayed. Steve Jobs and Martin Luther King, Jr. were betrayed before seeing their next level, and of course, Jesus was betrayed. Have you read their stories? I encourage you to do so.

Betrayal comes with the territory. Not everyone will understand who you are, your call, your mission, nor the gifts you possess. Because of this, they may mistreat, misjudge, misuse, malign, misspeak, undervalue, and talk about you. Do not expect others will have God's vision for who you are and what you are sent to do. Be ready to walk in the wisdom of God and hear who He wants you to align with to catapult you to your next. Otherwise, you may be setting yourself up for disappointment.

b. God is helping you build a stronger character.

As you reframe your circumstance, consider how you respond to betrayal or hurt. Your response will help (or hamper) building the character you need to sustain success at the next level. Use the hurt as an opportunity for character growth and self-assessment. Ask God to outline what you need to learn about yourself and your leadership skills. Be open and let Him teach you if there is a lesson to be learned.

c. God's rejection is your protection.

Sometimes betrayal, rejection, and mistreatment signal that the direction you are trying to go is not for you. Sure, you believe you are moving toward the vision God has given you, but at times, we can be limited in what we see. God is not. He sees your past, present, and future, and is always working it all for your good. (See Romans 8:28.) Thank Him for the yeses, open doors, and promotions, but also praise Him for the nos, dead ends, U-turns, and detours He puts before you to move you on to the right path, the path that leads not only to increase but also to peace, joy, and fulfillment. His protection from undue stress and drama we cannot see on the horizon, sometimes comes in the form of a hard no or even an offense from a person we least suspect.

2. Communicate your hurt.

Some people journal. Some cry out to God in prayer. Others go to a trusted friend, pastor, or licensed professional counselor. Still others do a combination of the three. Choose the method that works best for you. It is important to work through the hurt, so it does not stay lodged in your heart.

Unaddressed hurt can lead to unconscious and unhealthy judgments and generalizations which can cause trust issues and raise fears that hinder you from moving forward. The psalms of David give us a biblical example of one who poured His heart out before God, trusting Him with his healing, protection, and defense. Be honest in your journaling, prayers, or sharing. Healing can come when you are open with your feelings.

3. Forgive them.

Be ready to accept your responsibility for obeying God's command to forgive. As you may have learned, forgiveness is not initiated by an apology from the other party. Forgiveness starts with you. "Yes, God. I forgive them." No matter what was done to you, with God's help, you can forgive and let go of the offense.

One thing you need to know as you forgive is that reconciliation—restoration or continuation of the relationship—and forgiveness are not the same thing. If there is no change in behavior on the part of the offender—there is still abuse or misuse—it is wise to establish boundaries and maintain your distance.

Forgiveness is an internal heart action you take individually. Reconciliation takes cooperation of two or more parties to be successful, and to see full restoration of a relationship, trust first must be restored.

In some cases, forgiveness is a process. You may find yourself going back to God in prayer many times as you work with Him to release the feelings of bitterness and betrayal after you've been hurt. It may take time for you to truly release responsibility for their consequences into God's hands, and it may take time for you to get a revelation of God's perfect justice, which always has a fair outcome beyond what we see or sense.

You will know you have forgiven completely when thoughts of those who have offended you no longer cause feelings of fear, anger, or insecurity.

4. Forgive yourself.

Sometimes we blame ourselves for negative outcomes. We throw our own pity parties when things don't go the way we planned or when we've allowed certain people into our lives who go on to hurt us. But the forgiveness we extend to others, sometimes needs to be extended to ourselves. Let yourself off the hook for clouded vision or discernment. You won't always know the best way forward when you need to make a decision. You did the best you could with the knowledge available to you at the time. Look back to the first step in our prescription for forgiveness and know some setbacks are setups for your comeback. Commit to learn what you need to learn and do better the next time. Failure and disappointment are part of a life that is moving and doing.

5. Forgive God

This is a tricky one, because God is perfect. He does nothing wrong. However, in our finite minds, we sometimes blame God for the difficulties we experience in our lives and relationships. But here as with the other steps in the prescription, allow His Word and your time with Him to renew your perception of the Creator. God is faithful. He is love. He wants only good things for you. The things that happen to you are a result of your choices and the choices others make. While God will take those things and turn them around for your good, it breaks His heart when you are hurt, abused, or taken advantage of. His thoughts toward you are good and not evil. He loves you with an everlasting love. Release Him from any blame for causing bad things to happen in your life and watch your relationship with Him soar to new heights. Watch how you begin to feel His love and care for you. Begin to see you are not alone, that He is always with you, clearing the way for His glory to shine through you.

5. Reestablish trust.

We've looked at the weapons the enemy forms against iconic leaders. We've seen the toxic results of isolation and trust issues. We've also looked at ways to heal these broken places inside a leader's heart. Now it is time to restore the broken pathways and the avenues by which the favor, increase, and promotion of God can flow into your life. Restoring trust between others and you ultimately begins with building an unshakable faith in God. By what we have uprooted and dismantled in this chapter, I pray you are able to arrive at a point wherein you can confidently say,

> The LORD is on my side;
> I will not fear.
> What can man do to me?
> The LORD is for me among those who help me;
> Therefore I shall see my desire on those who
>   hate me.

Nine Spirits That Break the Eikonic Leader and How to Beat Them

> It is better to trust in the Lord
> Than to put confidence in man.
> —Psalm 118:6–8

May I challenge you to take this a few steps further? Would you make the following declarations with me today?

The Lord is on my side; I trust He is making a way for me.

The Lord is on my side; I will not doubt He is preparing the right people with whom I can accomplish His plans and purposes.

The Lord is on my side; I will wait for Him to lead me in the way I should go.

The Lord is on my side; I believe He will deal justly on my behalf.

The Lord is on my side; I believe He will order my steps and direct my path.

The Lord is on my side; I will not fear. His plans always work in my favor.

The Lord is on my side; I will believe He will give me wisdom and empower me to work excellently with others as well as have the time I need to excel alone—just Him and me.

Your Oxygen Mask

1. Of the nine demonic spirits that may come against iconic leaders, which of these have you wrestled with? What have you done (or what are you doing) to overcome them?

2. What flaws do you perceive within yourself? Are you transparent about these? Have you allowed them to discourage you or have you stayed focused on your purpose and mission?

3. What can you do to give grace and encouragement to yourself to mitigate the impact of your perceived flaws on your ministry, business, career and relationships?

4. Do you find it easy to forgive others? Yourself? What additional things can you do to strengthen your ability to forgive as God commands us to do?

Chapter 3

AN UNCONVENTIONAL INDIVIDUAL

ONE OF THE more admired and frustrating characteristics of an iconic leader is their fierce individuality. The iconic leader is well aware of the team dynamic but simply prefers to work alone. They know themselves well. They understand their limitations and the sacrifices they will submit to in order to get something accomplished. With all sincerity, they don't know whether anyone else is up to the task at the required level and they don't trust anyone else to subject themselves to the high standard of excellence that absolutely must be given. Simply put, the iconic leader trusts themselves and is willing to go through whatever it takes to get the job done. Will anyone else be this committed? They simply cannot imagine anyone else will.

Whether you have been in a leadership position or not, I am sure you have been told it is good to be a team player. However, iconic leaders generally loathe working in groups. It is not that they do not understand the benefits to be derived from group work and its purpose in the organization, they just prefer to work alone.

This preference to work alone stems from their inability to

trust others to carry out a project or task. This is not to say they think others cannot do the same things; they trust themselves more than they trust others.

You may recall early times in your life when this trait first began to show itself. Maybe you were the group member who did all the group work in school and now you are the employee who prefers to take on all the heavy lifting for work projects.

This is not to say an iconic leader will go through life never trusting others. Quite the contrary! When an iconic leader finds people who connect to the vision, understand how to operate cooperatively with their personality, and can deal with constructive feedback, they love to work with them. But for us, trust is earned after testing and successfully passing the test. Because iconic leaders expect excellence, it only takes one mistake to lose that trust.

Because you prefer to work alone, you will from time to time feel all alone, like a person in a foreign land. You are different than everyone around you, and because they consider you a know-it-all, you are often left out of social activities.

The Trap of Isolation

Let me issue this caution: though iconic leaders thrive when working on projects and developing strategies alone, God intends for you to be in relationship with others. When you are in isolation, nobody is speaking back to you but yourself, and that can be dangerous. The Bible says there is wisdom in a multitude of counselors. We will talk in a bit about how you can form that small multitude of trustworthy individuals, but always be mindful you need the perspective, wisdom, encouragement, and support of others.

What happens when you are in a tough season and lacking anyone you trust, all you speak to yourself is negativity? I'll tell you. You will put yourself at greater risk for unproductivity, lack of vision, or worse, depression. If you feed negativity with negativity, it grows. If you feed negativity with positive connection, words of wisdom, and encouragement, it dies.

Just as you have developed a discipline for hard work and are able to gain keen insight and ideas even when everyone else is worn out, connection and relationship will require a similar conscious effort and discipline, especially since doing so is not your default behavior. But you can do it. You must. You cannot leave room for the enemy here. He wants you to believe the lies he puts in your head that you can trust no one but yourself. He wants to isolate you and make you more susceptible to the nine spirits we discussed in the last chapter.

Isolation, which is really an extreme form of self-reliance in the context of iconic leadership, also can lead to pride and arrogance. You are not an island. You need both God and community. They will keep you humble and teachable, in a place where the grace of God is maximized to empower you to do great things.

Personality Complexities That Contribute to Being Misunderstood

It is hard for many to figure out the personality or leadership style of the iconic leader. Because of the iconic leader's multiple talents and high standard of excellence, they are often misunderstood and mistaken for being cocky. When the work others do is not accepted because it does not match the excellent quality or innovation characteristic of the iconic leader's work, the iconic leader is often perceived as arrogant. It is hard for others to figure out the personality or leadership style of the iconic leader. They are often viewed as complex individuals.

The iconic leader has a low tolerance for passive-aggressive behavior because he or she is very direct and to the point. Very outspoken and displaying a low tolerance for beating around the bush, an iconic leader can seem abrasive and may hurt the feelings of others. However, for the iconic leader, it is nothing personal. In a state of creating or strategizing, the iconic leader is focused on the idea and its outcome over the people with whom they are creating. When their abrasiveness is brought to their attention, they are quick to soften.

Loner in Love

Another area where our unconventional nature stands out is in our intimate relationships. The iconic leader generally is the tower of success in every sphere of their life. However, when love and romance are involved, personal relationships can get very complicated for the iconic leader. Whether the relationship involves two iconic leaders or just one, several pitfalls may arise. Below I share some of those pitfalls and how each partner can survive them.

Difficulty extending trust

As I uncovered in the last chapter, the iconic leader prefers to work alone, not because they do not value the input of others, but because it is hard for them to trust. In a competitive workplace, this personality characteristic can sometimes prove fruitful. However, love relationships thrive on trust. For the iconic leader, it can take a while before he or she lets go and begins to build trust in a relationship.

At the beginning of the relationship, trust issues can be a huge pitfall. However, the iconic leader in the relationship has no desire to remain at this stage and will learn to trust over a period of time. The noniconic partner, in this case, will need an extra dose of patience and willingness to understand as this trust builds.

The key to making the relationship work is to continue to create opportunities to encourage the development of that trust.

Challenges with communication and connection

From time to time, every relationship will experience misunderstanding—it is the nature of human interaction. The iconic leader possesses a complex and multifaceted personality that creates fertile ground for misunderstandings.

The iconic leader's individualism, demand for excellence, and direct personality are often interpreted by their significant other as selfishness, self-righteousness, and arrogance. Emotional intelligence plays a critical role in helping those in an iconic relationship survive this pitfall. The iconic leader must understand their personality can elicit negative emotions from their partner. Likewise, a partner must understand the complexity of the iconic leader is not designed to carry out intentional hurt. If the two can meet in the middle, the relationship can work.

Unmet expectations

The iconic leader has a high standard of excellence and generally exhibits an urgency for results. This can pose a problem in a relationship, as the noniconic partner may find it difficult to live or keep up with their iconic partner. This will result in unmet expectations on both sides.

This pitfall is one the iconic leader must pay close attention to if they are serious about building a relationship. Drawing a line between workplace or ministry expectations versus those in the relationship can help the couple to overcome this issue.

All relationships take work from those involved. However, when the extraordinary personality of the iconic leader is thrown into the mix, the pitfalls I mention above can kill a love relationship in the early stages. The iconic leader possesses one of the most misunderstood personalities, especially when that person is ignorant of their iconic labeling. Accordingly, it is important to take the opportunity to find out more about the characteristics of the iconic leader before starting a relationship.

The marriage of two icons

When two high-functioning, iconic leaders come together, we get the same as what happens when two type-A or strong personalities come together. These relationships can be hard to manage when one or the other won't decide to take the low road or the humble approach. Many times, these leaders connect because they have so much in common, but these types of relationships can be very demanding and exhausting. Generally, these leaders are in high demand at the workplace or within a ministry organization and they love to be part of the energy of what's happening. As such, they don't often take time for themselves—and by extension, they don't take time for each other or their relationship. Both people find themselves constantly lacking the affection and nurturing they so desire, leaving space for the enemy to enter and cause discord.

At the onset of an iconic union, passions run deep, and these two iconic leaders view romance and intimacy like a new project to conquer. Once they reach a level of bliss and fulfillment and other more demanding assignments come up, each may find themselves slowly neglecting their partner's need as well as their own.

One way this iconic pair can avoid the trap of intimate isolation is setting dates and appointments with each other, making time to connect with each other emotionally and physically. The iconic leader in them will honor this commitment as each of them makes the other part of their success routine. They must recall the blessing of being loved and desired and how that shapes their confidence and worth in every task they set out to accomplish outside of their union.

Another thing the couple can do is learn each other's love languages and apply it them appropriately. The five love languages, defined by Christian counselor and pastor Dr. Gary Chapman are:

1. Words of affirmation—using words to build up the other person. "Thanks for taking out the

garbage." Not "It's about time you took the garbage out. The flies were going to carry it out for you."

2. Gifts—a gift says, "He/she was thinking about me. Look what he/she got for me."

3. Acts of service—Doing something for your spouse you know they would like. Cooking a meal, washing dishes, vacuuming floors are all acts of service.

4. Quality time—by which I mean, giving your spouse your undivided attention. Take a walk together or sit on the couch with the TV off—talk and listen to one another.

5. Physical touch—holding hands, hugging, kissing, and sexual intercourse are all physical expressions of love.[1]

The five love languages identify how a person gives and receives love. When the iconic pair learn how each other receives love and each gives it in that way, they demonstrate that their significant other's needs are important to them. They will be better equipped to provide their partner with the connection they need, not what they think their partner wants. To learn more about the five love languages, visit the website www.5lovelanguages.com.

The iconic leader may be one of the more challenging of the leadership types when it comes to attracting and sustaining lifelong love relationships, but with intentional effort and a healed heart, it is very possible to thrive in marriage. You do not have to accept the status quo in this area of your life. You have the power of God on your side. You can break the "loner in love" label and become iconic in love. Isolation, especially in the first covenant God established at the beginning of time, is not His perfect design for you. Use the spiritual tools we discussed in the last chapter and know God will heal every hurt, insecurity, and fear. Every place in your soul where love has been sidelined, He will bring forward, and you will become the empathetic and connected spouse your partner needs you to be.

Breaking the Saul Mentality

One of the more troubling examples of a leader plagued by trust issues is found in the account of the Israelite king, Saul. His story is told in 1 Samuel 8 through 31. Though Saul had an anointed beginning, his ending was humiliating and disgraceful. This is not the destiny arc for an iconic leader God has in mind. It is our responsibility, however, to learn from Saul, and others who have gone before us, to take what they did well and apply it to our lives as well as understand what did not go well and work not to repeat those same mistakes.

Saul was anointed as king of Israel after the people demanded the prophet Samuel give them a king. Saul came in with a few insecurities. First Samuel 9:21 shows us where Saul questions his worthiness for being chosen: "Am I not a Benjamite, of the smallest of the tribes of Israel, and my family the least of all the families of the tribe of Benjamin? Why then do you speak like this to me?" Feeling small and insignificant pushed Saul into a position of trying to be big, significant, and self-reliant. Move after move, he made decisions as if he were trying to say, "I am not small. I matter. I can make good decisions. I am not weak. I am so strong and capable I don't need any advice or input from anyone. I'll show you what I am worth."

His insecurities led to jealousy and distrust of everyone around him. If you are familiar with the story, you recall how his distrust and jealousy of David drove him mad. (See 1 Samuel 17:57–18:16.) Many times, he tried to kill David, yet at the same time, he needed someone like David on his side. (See 1 Samuel 19–24.) The manifestation of wanting to do things his way or on his own also led Saul into disobedience to God, so much so that he lost the kingdom. (See 1 Samuel 13:1–15:33.)

This is not God's plan for the iconic leader. Distrust, self-reliance, and isolation are the enemy's traps for a worthy leader whose unique style and capabilities are hard to find in any other type of leader. Don't let Satan use rejection, fear, deception, or any other weapons to render you unproductive or ineffective. Your gifts and calling are integral to all God wants to do in the Earth, both in the marketplace and in the kingdom.

After some of what you have been through and with being so different, you may have a hard time believing, as Saul did, that God has called you out for a specific purpose. You may have been told you think you are all that, that you cannot keep friends, or that you cannot work well with others, but you are iconic. You can learn what you need to learn to elevate your God-given purpose over your natural proclivities. You are teachable and are able to rebound. I wrote this book to encourage you toward this awareness. I want to show you who you truly you are. I want to inspire you. I want to show you that you are not alone. There are more leaders like you, and we need you—and every iconic leader like you—to be confident and highly functioning in their right place.

As you begin to see yourself through the eyes of the Creator, you will see how He intends for you to make yourself available to others so His plans will be accomplished. You do not need to worry about compromising or making yourself more appealing to others in inauthentic ways. He will show you the fullness of your design and how to use it to bring the people and assignments you engage with to a whole new level. He will show you with whom you are to join forces. They will be people who celebrate you.

Only a select few, your tribe will be those who join you in challenging the status quo. Like you, what sets them apart is their focus and mission, which sometimes causes them to fly in the face of current traditions and leadership.

It doesn't matter what name you give them, your tribe consists of your people, your community, your family, your clan, your posse, your network, your circle. They come totally and completely out of the box, seeing new ways and perspectives from old, entrenched viewpoints while speaking to one's potential and not one's pain.

Like a gust of wind, our tribe organically flows to us by way of the mission or vision alone. Divinely assigned to align with and run in purpose with us, they may be local, regional, national, or global.

This divine connection may not make sense to you on a human level, yet you and your tribe are drawn to one another.

With these followers, your voice and message resonate, like a fresh intake of oxygen, inspiring them to move beyond limits they have set for themselves…and limits others have placed upon you all.

Your Oxygen Mask

1. What makes you unconventional? How has your individualism affected your relationships with others? What can you do to operate as your authentic self yet be mindful of your impact on others?

2. Have you ever felt isolated or alone? When you feel this way, what are some steps you can take to reconnect with community or with God?

3. Are you in an intimate relationship? Are your needs and the needs of your partner being met? Do you know your partner's love language(s)? Do you make time for the relationship just as your do for working on your purpose and mission? What steps can you take in this area today to build up and enhance your relationship?

4. Do you feel as though you need to prove your worth to others? What types of scenarios or situations trigger these feelings? What do you need to change about your self-perception so that you see yourself as the Creator sees you?

Chapter 4

BUILDING YOUR EIKONIC CIRCLE OF TRUST—YOUR TRIBE

A PASTOR FRIEND of mine has an incredibly neat and simple way to categorize the right people we need in our lives. He models his suggestions after the personalities and characteristics of some of the early church giants named in the New Testament. He says, "Everyone needs at least three people in their lives":

1. A Paul—someone who is just a little older in the faith. They are your sounding board and mentor. You can learn from their experiences.

2. A Barnabas—someone who is beside you and is in a place similar to where you are in life, so you can share the journey together.

3. A Timothy—someone you can invest in, encourage along the way, and bless with your God-given experience. Timothies will hold you accountable to live what you teach.[1]

Now, let's look at how to choose people who fit into these three categories, and maybe even expand the definitions a bit based on what we learn from the iconic leadership displayed in the life of Christ.

Who Would Jesus Choose?

One of my favorite illustrations of how a leader can choose the right tribe comes from John Gray, a well-known author and pastor. He talks about how Jesus, the ultimate iconic leader, selected His disciples.[2] He calls it the Principle of the Eight, the Three, and the One.

Throughout Jesus's ministry, there were many beyond the Twelve who followed Him which He did not select to occupy space in His inner circle. Even among the Twelve, only three were taken places the others were not invited. He had an inner circle within His inner circle. Those He called personally were not the same as those who followed Him voluntarily.

Only the three went with him to the inner court which was the Garden of Gethsemane; eight were left behind. Judas had already made his decision and had gone to close his deal with the Jewish religious leaders.

At the most critical moments, as a leader, you need to be able to discern who everybody is in your life. You need no unintentional relationships in the season in which you are being pressed and prepared for your ultimate assignment. Assess the relationships you have and put them in the category of an eight, a three, or a one. Who are your three? For Jesus, it

Building Your Eikonic Circle of Trust—Your Tribe

was Peter, James, and John, the three who went forward with Him to the next level.

Jesus outlines for us what it looks like to choose the right people who can go with you to the next level. Everyone can't go, and that's OK.

The Eight represent those who need to stay in the outer court. The Three represent those who can accompany you to the inner court. These were the people He knew to whom He could unveil Himself. A critical point for the iconic leader is this: if anyone could carry out His mission alone, it was Jesus. Yet, He chose to carry out His mission in community with others.

Despite what you think you can do, iconic leader, there are no successful Christian islands. Yes, you must be comfortable being alone at times because you need time to refresh and rejuvenate for your mission. Yes, it is important to recognize that certain things can only be done by yourself, but you also need the skills and feedback from your tribe. Certain periods or assignments may require you to be alone, obviously, but you cannot live life in sustained isolation.

Natural predators go after the isolated prey first. Even if you are wounded, the safest place is around other people in your tribe. The enemy can't do anything because he can't get to you. You are surrounded. Everybody has a limp or an issue. Your tribe or community covers you. They have your back and stand against the enemy on your behalf, saying, "Devil, I wish you would."

Peter, James, and John were always with Jesus at pivotal times of change and elevation in His ministry. God always wants us to be surrounded by people who will remind us of our ultimate destination.

When you are battling a season of vulnerability, you need to place yourself in the presence of your Peter, James, and John. You may love The Eight, but The Eight can't always see you unveiled. You have to be wise as a leader.

When it's OK to go alone

At the beginning of this chapter, I cautioned you against falling into isolation. There is a place an iconic leader must be ready to go to when necessary to restore strength and uncompromising stability in God. That place is solitude. There are times when neither your spouse nor your inner circle can be with you. There are some things only you and God can accomplish.

It is OK to be called away to a quiet place with God, a place where He speaks His plans and revelation to you. In solitude with God is where He does His deepest work in your heart, pressing out what is not like Him and pouring in those things that are, that you may attract the right people and opportunities aligned with His plans for your life. You should welcome those moments or seasons of solitude. It is God wanting you all to Himself.

I have heard some leaders call this place "the holy of holies." Comparing our alone times with God to the most holy place is done based on understanding we are the temple of God. His Spirit dwells within us, and when He is ready to do a deep work within us, preparing us for our most holy call, it seems appropriate to envision ourselves coming in from the outer courts of our everyday lives and entering the most holy place where His manifest presence resides. This is a time God ordains when an iconic leader knows they must enter this place alone.

Five Characteristics of the Ideal Iconic Tribe

Every leader cannot understand the deepest places of your heart, and that's OK. They won't all make it to the inner court and that is OK too. You don't have time to waste. God is launching you! When you launch into rare atmosphere, you can't have dead weight. So, let go of those who you thought should have been with you. Embrace those who are with you, and go on to the next level.

Beyond identifying your eight, three and one, here are some other characteristics that make up the ideal tribe for you as an iconic leader:

1. Your tribe is peculiar.

Your tribe will tend to look a lot like you, a group of similar misfits. Presenting as loners and often misunderstood, they will appear as non-conformists, rebellious and likely to buck authority.

2. Your tribe is looking for you.

Your energy naturally draws others to you. You don't need to go searching for followers. They will find you.

3. Your tribe will connect to your voice.

Your message will sound familiar to their souls, resonating and stirring purpose within them. It will be like an invitation, much like when Mary visited her cousin Elizabeth. Upon hearing Mary's voice, the baby in her cousin's womb leapt (Luke 1:41). Have you ever asked why Jesus would look at a fisherman like Peter, say, "Follow me," and Peter would up and leave everything to go with Jesus? There was something distinct about the voice Peter heard that resonated with something deep inside him. Jesus's invitation stirred up a reality Peter may have been ignoring all his life, that he indeed was called for a higher purpose. The voice of Jesus activated that purpose within him. You don't have to labor to get others to connect with you. Just speak.

4. Your tribe seeks transformation.

Since the assignment of an iconic leader is "to strategically influence the human element for the purpose of transformation toward an ideal, cause, or vision," those who connect with you will be there primarily for the purpose of moving from a stalled position to a place of potential. They will need someone who can speak to their destiny and challenge them to navigate beyond their pain, thereby moving into that potential. Like David and his mighty men of valor, they will look to you to act as a change agent in their lives—waking their spirit and bringing them out of Abdullam (1 Sam. 22).

They will see something in you they don't have, but they desire. As an iconic leader, you are the personification of the future for those who follow you. Iconic leaders actually experience a future reality and it is from that place you speak to your tribe and say, "Come up here."

5. Your tribe is collaborative.

The tribe is full of people who celebrate your wins and cry with you when you're hurting, the ones who will gladly wake up at the crack of dawn to take you to the airport, and those who you can't help but be yourself around, laughing, until you can't breathe.

They utilize their voice through many funnels—social media platforms, speaking engagements, workshops and mastermind groups, online, etc.—constantly looking to network with others with a similar voice or sound that speaks to their spirits. They look to identify with those who serve the same mission as you, reaching out to see if there are ways you and those others can support one another.

Attachment Versus Connection

An affirming quality comes with followership. There is also a critical need to be aware of those in your tribe who simply are attached to you, as opposed to those who are truly connected to you and your message. Remember, even Jesus had His Judas, one of the Twelve. The Bible never says Jesus approached Judas and told him to follow Him, as He did with Peter and others. In essence, Judas was attached to Jesus, and though he had a role to play that ultimately moved Christ into fulfilling His purpose, he was not intimately connected to Christ's purpose. In order to identify the Judases among you, you must try the spirit by the spirit (1 John 4:1–5).

Like a water hose connected to a faucet, someone who is only attached and not connected, will draw from the group without depositing anything of value. On the other hand, much like branches on a tree, the members who are connected to your vision will not only benefit from being part of the tribe, but also will contribute to its mission and growth. They will bear good fruit (Matt. 7:16–17).

It is for this reason, as an iconic leader, you cannot focus on numbers...as if the higher the number of followers (or likes), the more your mission or sense of self is validated. Like Jesus, you must know those among whom you labor (1 Thess. 5:12). Jesus was neither surprised nor deterred by the actions of Judas. His self-esteem was not wrapped up in nor dependent upon the opinions and perspectives of others.

> **Don't depend on your number of followers or "likes" to validate you. Remember, Hitler had millions; Jesus had twelve. It's about making an impact for today; it's about leaving a legacy for tomorrow.**

The reality, at times, is people will come with their own agenda and attempt to attach or connect themselves to you and/or the group for the sole purpose of morphing or bending it to achieve or accomplish their personal vision or goal. Judas Iscariot was a perfect example of this.

Some members of the group may be engaged for the long

haul, even a lifetime. Other relationships may be seasonal, meant only for a specific time and purpose. Examples of this include:

- A mentee there to learn, and then transition into the assignment God has for them

- A God-ordained resource sent to supply the group with specific gifts and support for the task in front of them

- A mentor there to come alongside you and other members in the community to provoke, instill courage, or provide support through a particular phase or stage

The members of the tribe are called to a purpose, not a place, location, or group. Their assignment may have an expiration date. Nevertheless, this does not mean they are not loyal. In fact, seasonal group members are usually loyal to a fault and may have a difficult time leaving, even after hearing the Holy Spirit clearly tell them it's time to go.

It may be difficult for the leader to let them go, as well. However, as with the military, God assigns your purpose; you don't get to choose. The iconic leader may be re-assigned, and the followers as well, because, once the tribe has matured and gained the needed lessons or training, they are now ready to operate in their own assignments.

How to Expand Your Tribe

When God begins to shift you into large realms of influence, you may feel Him encouraging you to expand your tribe. As you grow, you may need more hands on deck to help you accomplish the vision God has given you. Here are some ways to do that.

Network

Put yourself out there. Go to different events and meet new people. It's time to say, "Yes" to social events, morning coffee meetings at Starbucks, and those invitations to parties and dinners. It is time to accept those invitations and communicate. Start cultivating those friendships that you have been neglecting or not nurturing and let them know you are open to developing true and solid relationships with them. Make sure you are likeminded with them and they possess the same morals and value systems as you.

Every opportunity you get to meet new people, say yes. You never really know the full impact of your influence with others until you pursue it.

Be open

Because the iconic leader tends toward isolationism and going it alone at work, they may not gravitate toward others socially either. Being part of a tribe or community takes an investment of time, participation, and attention. Check the newsletters of local museums or cultural groups for unique opportunities. Take a language course together as a family. Start a multicultural book club. Get creative!

Continue to be transparent, making time for people, and watch your relationships with them quickly take root. When you find someone who belongs in your tribe, there will be an emergence of creativity and things will begin to flow as if from behind a door that suddenly has been unlocked. You will find your purpose.

Cover new ground

Travel is essential, and I'm not just talking about expensive journeys to new parts of this country and beyond. Start in your own city.

If money is a factor, there are all kinds of inexpensive and complimentary events. Check your social media and newspaper. As I stated above, try visiting new parks, museums, and restaurants outside of your own community.

If you have a friend of a different culture, ask to join them on some of their events or accept their invitations and enjoy the diversity of culture and what your own city has to offer. Meet new people by joining a new club or trying out a new hobby.

QUALITY OVER QUANTITY

Many iconic leaders begin with a pure heart after God's heart, only to end up with painful disappointments, ruthless criticism, and rejection. Your tribe will not be perfect individuals. They simply are focused on a specific goal, as are you, and everyone within the tribe has something of value to push the vision forward.

So, never be above learning from and working with your tribe. Also, don't get hung up on how many are following you (or even, how many leave). It's not the quantity of people in the group; it's the quality of the relationships. The number doesn't demonstrate how iconic your leadership is; the purpose and depth of your impact does.

You will know your tribe because they will look like you, and when you find them, your voice will be amplified and appreciated. Your tribe will be the light bringers, the world shifters, and the trailblazers. Not only will you nurture their growth and transformation, you will be supported by them as well. They will celebrate you and not just tolerate you. They are not afraid of your change and success.

So, those who don't get it weren't meant to. Just keep doing that thing God has placed in your heart to do.

Whether for a season or a lifetime, the iconic leader is responsible for being mindful of those within their sphere of influence, so once you've identified your tribe, continue to operate in humility and grace.

> From whom the whole body fitly joined together and compacted by that which every joint supplieth, according to the effectual working in the measure of every part, maketh increase of the body unto the edifying of itself in love.
>
> —Ephesians 4:16, kjv

Your Oxygen Mask

1. Have you identified your tribe? Where did the members of your tribe come from? What unique skills do they bring to help move you forward toward the vision and purpose God planted in you?

2. Do you know your Eight, Three and One? Who are those among you who are part of your inner circle? What is it about them that defines them as such?

3. Are you nurturing your tribe? What are you doing to grow and develop them for their own missions as they support you in yours?

4. How well do you handle when members of the group depart? Do you celebrate them and wish them well or do you resent them or take it as a personal failing? How can you exemplify your understanding before the tribe that some memberships are but for a season?

5. How have you extended yourself to identify and grow your tribe? In what new and different ways will you seek to connect with likeminded individuals going forward?

Chapter 5

CHURCH, CAN YOU HANDLE ME?

It's Sunday morning, and you're sitting in church. The worship leader is up leading the band in a high-spirited praise song. The volume and the energy levels are through the roof. On one side someone's jumping up and down shouting various praises. On the other side, someone is bent over, arms outstretched, and audibly weeping. In the aisles, several are shouting and running while others are jumping and singing in the rows. Still others raise hands, heads back and lifted toward heaven.

The pastor marches back and forth across the front of the church, compelling everyone with a loud voice to go deeper: "He is worthy. Don't hold back. Give Him all the praise He deserves. I feel Him moving in this place. Oh, come on! You can do better than that. He is worthy!"

The whole room erupts into an even higher level of praise.

"I don't know about you," the pastor interjects, "but I'm not going miss out on what God is doing in this place. I'm not going to let the rocks cry out for me."

And higher still, the music and the praise and worship soar. Everyone is in—everyone, but you.

Does this seem familiar? Have you ever been in a moment like this? You feel somewhat awkward—almost like you've stepped outside of yourself. Maybe on another day you would have been the person weeping with their hands outstretched. But on this day, something is not quite the same. You may have tossed the thought back and forth in your mind that perhaps you aren't as spiritual as everyone around you. Everyone else is being touched by this move of God, why aren't you?

With no judgment intended, you open an inner query: "This can't be all there is to the move of God. Here we are in these four walls...What will all the shouting do for us? How many of us will really refuel and head out from here to change the world?"

You respond to the volley of thoughts in your head that you love God, you love His presence, and if He were not trying to call you higher to see something from a different perspective, you too may have been all in. But something different is happening with you. You feel it confirmed in your spirit, so you submit and allow Him to speak.

As an iconic leader, you can't help but to see the gaps, the needs, and the missing links. It is not that you are negative; it is that you are specially wired to strategize and home in on the logistics and effective systems necessary to produce a higher level of results. It's who God made you to be. You are wired to see the hidden potential and greatness lurking in a ministry or organization. You see both the challenges and opportunities. Your extraordinary sight gives you the ability to hope against hope and believe despite the odds that the challenges can be easily overcome and the opportunities easily seized. But then, as you express your high-powered vision and optimism to other leaders and decision makers, you are perceived as critical and rebellious, and that stings.

Why Iconic Leaders Are Leaving Ministries

There is a group of iconic leaders sitting in churches today, experiencing just what I describe above. They are completely frustrated. They love Jesus and His people, yet they are having a hard time fitting their gifts and talents into the kingdom. As a ministry leader and professional coach, I have worked with iconic leaders who struggle with utilizing their gifts and skills in ministry. Iconic leaders are often misunderstood, and their strong personality can lead to discomfort even among Christians. Because the iconic leader needs to operate in an environment of excellence, they will leave any organization that does not embrace their talents and skills.

The Christian community now faces a high volume of individuals leaving ministry because of "church hurt." This includes the iconic leader. We're going to look now at four reasons why iconic leaders are exiting ministry within the four walls of the church.

1. They don't fit in.

Iconic leaders struggle to find their place within traditional church culture. Their gifts and talents are often outside of the norm. Accordingly, mainstream Christians fail to recognize or utilize these gifts, which leads to the iconic leader feeling ignored and ostracized. The Bible says a person's gift will make room for them (Prov. 18:16). When this does not happen, the iconic leader typically will leave.

2. They are disconnected.

Leaders in the fivefold ministry—apostles, prophets, evangelists, pastors, and teachers—have a hard time connecting with the iconic leader. Iconic leaders are known for their high demand for excellence and generally possess a variety of gifts. They are also very direct in their utterances and many leaders find it hard to keep up with the iconic leader's need for urgency. The inability of other church leaders to understand and embrace the dynamic personality of the iconic leader results in a disconnect. Oftentimes this disconnect is subconscious, but over time, it will cause the iconic leader to leave the church.

3. They lack support.

Iconic leaders, by their personality traits, appear healthy and whole. Those who they lead and even those who lead them assume the iconic leader has everything together and not in need of support. However, this is far from the truth. Iconic leaders often go through extreme warfare throughout their lives and carry around a huge weight. Their iconic disposition may not allow them to ask for help. If church leaders and others are not able to discern the need for help and support, the iconic leader will leave.

4. They have a ministry unto themselves.

God gives iconic leaders a ministry and brand that is different than most. Their unique display of talents and gifts can intimidate another leader. Ministry leaders find it hard to understand the calling of the iconic leader because it does not fit the mold. To add to this, iconic leaders are very guarded and do not open up readily to enable others to better understand them. In the absence of true understanding of the ministry of the iconic leader, feelings of abandonment cause the iconic leader to leave the church.

Ministry life is important to the iconic leader. However, with little understanding on the part of those in church leadership, the iconic leader may find it hard to use his or her gifts and talents to grow the body of Christ. Iconic leaders are extraordinary in their personality and leadership style. They need extraordinary mentoring to ensure they can contribute to ministry work.

The Right Leader Sees the Iconic Leader for Who They Are

If you think about it, zeal and rebellion look almost like the same thing when viewed from the wrong vantage point. It takes a special leader to see the hidden gem within an iconoclast. They will see that you are not rebellious, that you are visionary, daring, a breaker of traditions and the status quo—for a purpose. They will see you are different.

While those who are given to the traditions of men will disregard, devalue, and try to silence you and your expression of God almost immediately, the leaders who want to see God unleashed in their ministries and communities in a new and refreshing way will see you for who God made you to be and will commit to refine you and come alongside your vision. God is establishing apostolic leaders who are open with their life experiences and platforms. Whether or not they are iconic themselves, they are not intimidated by iconic leaders who come with their critical eye, deep thinking, and dynamic style. They already know these leaders come needing a place to fit and function fully in their unique giftings, and also a place to be resuscitated.

The next move of God places iconic leaders at the center of transformation and the reclaiming of nations for the kingdom. Because of this, these special church and ministry leaders who are ready to receive iconic leaders will sit down at the table and examine the challenges and opportunities facing the body of Christ with the iconic leader. They are ready to uncover godly strategies for leveraging resources within the body of Christ to carry out God's mission beyond the church's four walls. So, whether the church can handle you or not, the church needs you, and those forward-thinking, trailblazing church leaders exist with whom God will connect you.

The Iconic Leader Needs the Apostolic Leader

The apostolic leader is the ideal leader for the iconic leader. He or she understands the fivefold ministry, which is built upon the understanding that every person is different and has a different set of skills, talents, and abilities. Therefore, when they come into relationship with the iconic leader, they welcome them and their many gifts, and look for creative, influential, and change-making positions in which to place them.

Like apostolic leaders, iconic leaders thrive on new ways of doing things and seeing the world. Though they appreciate some structure, iconic leaders are most inspired when they don't feel bound by pre-established ways to get things done. Both apostolic and iconic leaders are visionaries. Once the details are ironed out, they are able to help carry another leader's vision through to completion. Iconic leaders work very well with leaders who have a sense of urgency. Likewise, apostles proceed through every assignment with urgency. Both understand the spiritual aspect of that urgency and are passionate about the kingdom.

Different than an iconic leader, an apostolic leader is people-driven. The apostolic leader knows this about themselves and is aware the iconic leader is more idea-driven. Therefore, the apostolic leader is able to relinquish authority to the iconic leader when their particular skillset or gifting is needed in order to accomplish the mission at hand. An apostolic leader brings in people and new initiates, open to finding new ways to design needed systems and structures. They are open to expansion and respond to challenges and problem-solving. This makes them great mentors and supporters of iconic leaders who like to set trends, create new inroads, and design the blueprints.

An Apostolic Nature

> And he gave some, apostles; and some, prophets; and some, evangelists; and some, pastors and teachers; for the perfecting of the saints, for the work of the ministry, for the edifying of the body of Christ.
> —Ephesians 4:11–12, kjv

Iconic leaders are natural servant leaders as they love to serve and help people. They are strong discerners and seers in the ministry, in the marketplace, and with those they mentor. Because of their ability to impact current agendas as well as implement new ones, it is easy to see how they are apostolic in nature.

What is the apostolic ministry?

The Greek word *apostolos* means "one sent forth."[1] The apostle's purpose is manifold:

- Reaching new territories (Rom. 15:20)

- Laying a firm foundation (1 Cor. 3:10–11)

- Training other leaders (Acts 14:21–23 and Titus 1:5)

- Problem-solving (Acts 6:1–7)

Although the apostolic ministry was established in the New Testament, the Word of God states the very church would be built on the foundation of the prophets *and* the apostles (Eph. 2:19–20). Why is this? Because prophets speak the heart and mind of God while apostles provide structure and order. Both of these giftings are abundant in the iconic leader.

Apostolic tribes

In chapter three, we discussed ways to identify and expand your tribe. In this chapter, we take a deeper dive into understanding how your tribe operates. Like you, it is also apostolic. This is why it is so important you are in proper alignment with those with whom God is trying to connect you.

Alignment is the proper positioning or state of adjustment of parts in relation to each other; a position of agreement or alliance.[2]

God is connecting and aligning you in order to accelerate and bring you into an intensified process of knowing who you are and what you are called to do. An apostolic tribe will help you unlock and tap into your calling. This is why God wants to disconnect someone or something from your life, even though you keep fighting it, desperately trying to force fit it.

Embrace the cleansing because next-level alignments often unlock next-level assignments.

> **Proper alignment is key in this next season of your life.**

A single apostle is not going to change a territory alone. It is the apostolic mantle of supernatural power on a group of people set in the family of God and running under the same mandate, mission, and commission that activates the alignment. But, how do you know if you are in alignment with your tribe?

When you, the iconic leader, are in right relationship with the members of your tribe, you all will be in agreement, fitly joined together, each joint supplying whatever is needed according to Ephesians 4:16. There will be a unity of purpose, motive, and identity. Areas of obscurity or confusion will come to light and into order seemingly overnight.

Everything will fit just right.

> A right alignment sharpens, accelerates, and refines you. A wrong alignment delays, dulls, and contaminates.[3]
> —Ryan LeStrange

Each of us have a different mantle according to the mandate, the assignment and role we are given, and each of us have varying degrees of anointing and authority within the given mandate. To that end, the apostolic mantle provides the ability to live beyond economic and social limitations and to defy the odds and overcome the obstacles.

The story of Joseph is a perfect example of one who didn't fit in yet defied the odds, overcame obstacles, and brought forth the purpose and plan of God (Gen. 50:20). Although Joseph is not necessarily thought of as an apostle, nor do we assign him the title, he was definitely apostolic in nature in the way he strategically established systems that saved the nation from the disastrous effects of a drought. He was also prophetic in nature as a seer and builder. He used his ability to discern, along with divine wisdom, to apply solutions to the problems he discerned.

Recognizing the signs of the forthcoming drought, Joseph advised the king of the steps needed to prepare for the coming season, then used his organizational skills to get the job done.

His extraordinary abilities, with respect to God and people, did not operate in separate domains. The genius of his success lay in the effective integration of his divine gifts and acquired competencies. For Joseph, all of this was godly work. Joseph was able to access Heaven's resources to provide for the nation of Egypt and the Jews during the seven-year season of famine.

When the Church Is Not Your Ministry

Though iconic leaders can find spiritual support within a church, the magnitude of some iconic leaders' assignments cannot be housed within the church. As I said at the beginning of the chapter, a generation of marketplace and ministry leaders are sitting in the church pews completely frustrated. They have gifts and talents but can't find any place in the church where their gifts and talents fit. Some of these leaders just need the right church leader to help them acclimate their fivefold ministry calling. Others' assignments simply are not meant for the church.

When Jesus launched His ministry, it wasn't for the four walls of a church, it was for the world. As He recruited His leadership team, He recruited people like physicians and fisherman. He didn't recruit preachers.

Then, as today, Jesus wasn't looking for ordinary leaders. Today, He's looking for creative, iconic leaders who don't do ministry as usual. These extraordinary leaders do ministry unusual. These leaders are designers, directors, playwrights, airline attendants, entrepreneurs, millionaires, billionaires, and change agents...anyone who will do their thing in all the Earth while being in the church.

There is a place in the world for you and your gifts. Just because you don't fit the "churchy stereotype" doesn't make you any less effective nor does it make you any less of a Christian.

Your gifts are needed. Stop waiting on permission to pursue your passion. Do what you were born to do.

Don't Despise Divine Alignment

What was required in the last season was only preparatory for you to have strength and endurance in this one. Therefore, don't despise what you went through as it was needed to make sure you were ready for this current season. Now that you are here, however, you will need apostolic wisdom and prophetic insight to navigate this new territory properly.

God will help you identify an apostolic father and/or mother who has a strong prophetic mantle and edge. He literally will connect you to apostolic teams, tribes, or networks in order to sharpen and protect His investment in you. Don't get distracted, discouraged, or disconnected to the vision God has placed in you. Gas up and press harder, deeper, and higher, and refresh and encourage one another because the enemy of our souls is after the alignment.

As it was for the apostles of the first century, your way may be unchartered, but the effort required to apply your unique gifts and mantle toward manifesting the divine vision set before you will be well worth it for generations to follow.

Your Oxygen Mask

1. Have you left a church or ministry because you felt as though you did not fit within those four walls? What prompted you to leave and do you have lingering "church hurt"?

2. Are you currently connected with a church or ministry? Do you struggle with finding your fit within that church or ministry?

3. In what ways does the leader of your church or ministry help or support you in your calling?

4. Are you familiar with the fivefold ministry, specifically the apostolic mantle? What characteristic traits do you possess as an iconic leader that align with the apostolic mantle?

Chapter 6

ANOINTED BUT UNANNOUNCED

ONE VERY CRITICAL thing for the iconic leader to grasp when it comes to walking in the fullness of their purpose is the timing of the Lord. Though discernment is high on the list of their giftings, sometimes patience is not. But heed this caution: there are seasons and positions where God has you in which you are anointed but not announced. If you want to please God and walk in His favor, you have to learn to be OK with being in this place for the time He establishes.

> Jesus turned the whole ministry thing upside down.... He was God when He was born. He was God at twelve years old. But He wasn't announced until He was thirty.[1]
> —John Gray

There is a time for everything under heaven, and there is the appointed time of God for the iconic leader to be released into their calling and destiny. You may have found yourself asking at various times throughout your life, "Why are they not calling my name? Why don't they know what I carry?" One of the best reasons I've heard for this comes from author and pastor John Gray. He says, "God does not give you a platform before He prepares you for it on the backside of the mountain...on the backside of the valley, in a meadow..."

We need to be careful what we pray for as platforms don't make us, but instead expose the inner motivations of our hearts. Jesus was in the Garden of Gethsemane, pressed into submitting to the Father's will for His life in that season. Gethsemane means oil press. It is the place of crushing. In our spiritual Gethsemanes, we are pressed and pressed until there is no skin, no pit, no seed. We are pressed until the only thing left is the oil, which represents the anointing of the Holy Spirit.

This place is a hard place. We can be so anxious for people to see our value, so we can be about our Father's business. The sense of urgency in iconic leaders doesn't like what they may see as "beating around the bush," but promotion and walking fully in their purpose and calling requires a time of pressing. We often hear this identified as "the process." As we transition from one level to the next, we must submit to the process. Expect that on your way out of the press, you won't look the same as when you entered. We cannot afford to take what we had in the last season into the next. Even what was good in the last season can be the very thing that holds us back from being catapulted to the next level with God in this season.

Another thing that can bring about angst—as you pray for

the next level, for promotion, or to get on with the work of your true destiny—is you just don't stumble into Gethsemane. You don't accidentally find Gethsemane. You are invited there. Can you wait on God to invite you into the next level? If you really want to go to the next level, let God invite you to Gethsemane. This is where He crushes your flesh, so the only thing left is the pure fragrant oil He wants people to smell when they encounter you. Your sweet-smelling oil will attract who is called to your life. As you have already discerned, you are not called to partner with or minister to everyone. Every church and leadership team are not for you to join. Every job offer is not for you to take. God has ordained a special place for you where they will relish in the fragrant oil the Holy Spirit has poured upon you.

> **There is a reckless remnant that will rise out of the glory of God. Their training will be unconventional and birthed out of their life experiences. They will be sharpened by spiritual leaders that flow out of love, grace, and wisdom. Holy Spirit will empower them, and they will keep their unpolished edge and carry power to push back the darkness in regions where no one else will go![2]**
> **—Ryan LeStrange**

When the Iconic Leader Is Finally Announced

As Lance Wallnau once prophesied, I too see coming an unnamed move of God with an anointing and flow man will not be able to brand. This type of move is geared toward iconic leaders who do not wish to draw attention to their many superior gifts, skills, and talents and who desire only to be effective and see the world transformed for the better.

In his teaching on "How the Seven Mountains Will Be Taken by Individuals Like You," Wallnau shares that believers "ought to be at the top of the religion mountain of influence."[3] Those seven mountains are:

1. Church

2. Family

3. Education

4. Government—law, military

5. Media

6. Arts

7. Business

Which means everyone's purpose cannot and will not be fulfilled inside the four walls of the church. Consider Joseph, who dressed and spoke like an Egyptian even in front of his brothers, who as a result, didn't know who he was. He did not seem like a Jew/Israelite at all. Look at Daniel, who stood before three or four consecutive kingdom administrations. He was educated in the schools of Babylon. He was a Babylonian scholar and wise man. The first chapter of Daniel gives us clues as to the divine talents and skills he and his friends possessed. He wisely knew how governments operate and had mastery of the language of the Chaldeans. (If you don't become a cultural interpreter of how to bring the kingdom of God by stealth into the kingdoms of this world, you won't be able to accomplish what Daniel actually did—He spoke like a Babylonian but thought like a Jew. He had the supernatural mind of Christ.)

When you operate with this level of wisdom, you don't need to tell people where you get your information from, except as appropriate. All honor belongs to God. Ultimately, you don't have to tell them how you do what you do. As Wallnau suggests, your goal as an iconic leader who serves in the everyday corporate or government sectors of our world, is to infiltrate, run silent, and run deep.

He goes on to say:

> In this next move of God, key leaders are going to emerge or be converted within the key mountains of influence. We will see that small becomes the new big. The Davids that God is raising up are small in stature or will not be as well-known compared to the more prominent and better-known people. In the hillside with a few sheep, God was preparing a young man for an assignment that would solve a giant national problem. You cannot determine the scope or size of your impact by the few sheep you might be working with right now.[4]

Wallnau explains how the prophet Samuel went into the business mountain to approach Jesse who owned sheep—the sheep were Jesse's business. On the hillside, Samuel anointed David. Sometimes church leaders get stuck thinking they have to do everything transformative in a culture, but that is not what we are seeing with Samuel. Wallnau said:

> Samuel's assignment was to anoint, confirm, and convince David that David had the authority to advance into a governmental position that would seek the well-being of a nation. Your primary objective is to bring into activation the emerging individuals who will be able to lock shields in high places and shift the environment.[5]

The church leader's assignment is to identify key people, support them, and come alongside them in their journey to influence the world.

As Wallnau says, a paradigm shift is a new context for what we already believe. The body of Christ needs to embrace the new paradigm that involves iconic leaders going out into the world fully supported, endorsed, and commissioned by their local church to transform the sphere of influence over which God has given them authority.

Getting an anointing within the four walls of the church strong enough to somehow filter out and influence culture was never the strategy. When Jesus said, "I still have many things to say to you, but you cannot bear them now" (John 16:12), He spoke not just to the first-century church. He was speaking to every church that is alive, telling them to get ready for a paradigm shift. As He spoke about that upgrade and that fresh utterance, it challenged, even to this day, every sacred tradition and expectation we have ever had. Just because we are a prophetic community does not mean we know when the prophecy is to be fulfilled.

When you think about it, Joseph, right up to the end, tried to negotiate his way out of his own prophecy, says Wallnau. Joseph didn't realize what he was doing was disastrous. What would have happened if his negotiation had worked and he got out of prison and went back to dad's house? Nothing he had been sent to do would have been accomplished. The land would have been ravaged by famine because there would have been no Joseph in Egypt to solve the problem.

This is how so many of our prophecies are misappropriated in the body of Christ. We interpret every vision, dream, and revelation within the context of the four walls. But this is where the iconic leader comes in—the change-makers, the innovators, the ideators…

Small Is the New Big

What if the church is not where you are supposed to be? What if you have been a prisoner of a prophetic process? You can begin to thank God that He hasn't delivered you by the authority of your utterances before now. Because when you show up at the right place at the right time, it's not about you. It's about the multitude you impact. Small is the new big. Individuals are shaping the masses. So little David has to get to the mountain of government, and God gets him there through the arts.

We talk about favor—the attraction of God to you that releases a supernatural influence through you so other people are inclined to cooperate with you in the prophetic assignment God gave you. If you are not in line with your prophetic assignment, why would God want to put a supernatural charisma around you? You won't need it.

God puts His favor on some of the most unlikely individuals, but that is because He looks on the heart and not the outward appearance. You may be one of the unlikely, a little ruddy and unruly to some, but God sees a fierce warrior in you who will not compromise when He sends you out into the marketplace. He sees one with a heart after His. So, don't wink at the small opportunities. You may not be able to see the great impact God is waiting to manifest through you as you say yes and go in with both feet to what He is calling you to do.

Expansion Comes with Pain

Your yes to God opens the door to exponential favor and expansion but know this too: expansion comes with risk. Expansion comes with danger. Expansion comes with upsetting the status quo. Expansion is not safe.

You're not the type who prays only, "Lord, keep me safe and lead me not into temptation." You pray daring, iconic prayers, "May God expand my borders," as Jabez did in 1 Chronicles 4:9–10. What iconic leaders know and need to stay knowing is that the second part of Jabez's prayer—that I may not cause pain—may not be what allows you to go against the grain and the traditions of men. There is something called growing pains that iconic leaders initiate with they are invited into an group or organization.

Anointed but Unnnounced

Iconic leaders don't pray, "Lead us not into temptation." They pray, "May God expand my borders and give me no pain." This is the essence of the prayer of Jabez in 1 Chronicles 4:9–10. What we want is a painless expansion of inheritance, but that is not how it works. What we can pray for is discernment to know whether the pains are growing pains or consequences of wrong or hasty actions. We can stop and pray about whether the next open door we stand in front of us is the right one. Sometimes we think the open door before us is God, but promotion can be premature.

This is the season wherein people who have been held back are going to discover they were held back so they could prepare to handle what they are about to step into. It wasn't God's denial. It was God's protection from the prayer we weren't praying, which was "Lead me not into temptation. Don't give me more than I can handle."

I'm in a place in my leadership journey where, once the revelation hit me that God had protected me by telling me no or wait, I have had to stop and thank God. To you, I say, rejoice when God orders your steps. Some of the hurts you've experienced were His grace and mercy surrounding you and leading you away from where you were to where you need to be—in the right place at the right time. Can you say amen to that?

Your Oxygen Mask

1. You have been anointed, but have you been announced? Have you sought promotion before

God says it's your time? Have you chafed against leadership and the church when in fact it is God who is holding you in order to prepare you for the next level?

2. Have you completed your season of pressing? Is there still more that God needs or requires of you? Will more pressing be required in the place where you are before only your sweet-smelling oil remains?

3. Do you possess the wisdom you need to go with stealth into and influence spheres outside of the church to bring the kingdom of God into those places? When you interact with these outside spheres, what challenges do you encounter?

Chapter 7

YOUR SECRET'S OUT

WHAT A JOURNEY so far! We started with uncovering the eight qualities that sum up the essence of who you, the iconic leader, are. We identified the demonic agents that come to render you ineffective and discussed strategies to remain on the offensive against their attacks. We also worked through the difficulties and challenges that may come as a result of your unconventional style and how you can harness empathy, flexibility, and forgiveness to receive help and uplift in your life.

We went on to examine how you fit within the church and what to do if you don't. Your ideal leaders, mentors, and tribe were also called out. We discovered there is a place for you, and when you come upon it, that ministry or church absolutely will be prepared and ready to handle you—and beyond that, they will celebrate you.

In sum, what we have done up to this point is empower and equip you for full-on service to the world and fulfillment of your iconic destiny. The principles discussed and areas of hurt that have been healed clear the way for you to come out of isolation and lose your fear of being rejected. Your healed, delivered, supported, and celebrated self can confidently stand at the front of what God is doing and shine!

I believe with God in you; you are not a secret to be kept. Let the secret out—you are iconic. God made you this way and He is pleased with you. Matthew 5:14–16 says this:

> You're here to be light, bringing out the God-colors in the world. God is not a secret to be kept. We're going public with this, as public as a city on a hill. If I make you light-bearers, you don't think I'm going to hide you under a bucket, do you? I'm putting you on a light stand. Now that I've put you there on a hilltop, on a light stand—shine! Keep open house; be generous with your lives. By opening up to others, you'll prompt people to open up with God, this generous Father in heaven.
> —The Message

Your confidence to shine brightly as an iconic leader looks a lot like God setting you on a high place, your "Yes, God, I'm ready!" and His, turning on the spotlight, "Action!"

My purpose in writing this book is to help you to discover this high place—what some may call your "sweet spot"—and to function in it at your best so you experience a fulfilling, well-balanced life, producing consistent, fruitful and satisfying results.

Now that you have a better grasp of who you are and why you've had such difficulty finding your fit, I want to use this chapter to give you some strategies on how to flourish within your fit.

Good stewardship is imperative to the iconic leader's ability to shine and flourish. You have to be very intentional about nurturing and guarding your unique and multifaceted gifts. Let's look at four techniques or principles to help you do this well:

1. Embrace

Embracing who you really are is very important to being free to function in the center and strength of your iconic identity. When you don't embrace who you are, you do not live authentically, and you constantly feel as though you are changing—a chameleon who seeks to meet the variable expectations that come across all your relationships. You don't want to become a people pleaser. In order for everything around you to truly thrive, you must be who you were designed to be rather than who everyone else is comfortable with. When you don't do this, nothing grows—not you, your gifts, nor your ministry or workplace results. You remember how we ended the last chapter—with expansion comes pain. Don't fear the purposeful friction that sometimes appears when you work through logistics with another leader.

Sometimes you have to wade through the chaos to get back to a place of peace and homeostasis, or equilibrium. Remain open, positive, and communicative. Don't shut down or shut out others. Voice your internal process by sharing with your team. You can use phrases that start with, "What I am thinking is…" or "What I am mulling over in my mind is this…" You even can involve others and open yourself up to constructive feedback by posing your thoughts as questions: "What do you think of this?" What do you think about our trying this?"

You know you have value, and you know others do as well. Use open-ended communication to help your shine come to the fore while creating room for others to do the same. Use your directness to keep your team focused on the main objective while framing any critical assessment with your special brand of positivity and hope.

By embracing your strengths as an ideator and creative leader, the energy of your true nature will push through. At your best, your iconic leadership style causes you to be very communicative and great at establishing relationships as your ideas take the lead. Utilize your toughness to your advantage. Apply it, properly framed within the context of the mental toughness needed to bring out some of those innovative ideas you have.

You have it in you to create environments wherein everyone can fit and flourish, where no one feels they need to walk on eggshells. Your tribe will feel your confidence in what you bring to the table and find relief in knowing where you are coming from rather than guessing.

2. Affirm

Affirmations are a very big part of who I am and how I nurture myself as well as guard against discouragement and lack of focus. I recommend you incorporate this daily practice of affirming yourself too.

According to the Positive Psychological Program, affirmations are "positive phrases or statements used to challenge negative or unhelpful thoughts."[1] Their benefits are scientifically proven, as shared by this group of experts from several studies. A major benefit of positive affirmations is how they affect our brains: "MRI evidence suggesting that certain neural pathways are increased when people practice self-affirmation tasks (Cascio et al., 2016). If you want to be super specific, the ventromedial prefrontal cortex—involved in positive valuation and self-related information processing—becomes more active when we consider our personal values (Falk et al., 2015; Cascio et al., 2016)."[2]

The experts highlight six benefits of daily positive affirmations:

1. Self-affirmations decrease health-deteriorating stress (Sherman et al., 2009; Critcher and Dunning, 2015).

2. Self-affirmations have been used effectively in interventions, leading to an increase in positive physical behavior (Cooke et al., 2014).

3. They may help with perception of otherwise "threatening" messages, including interventions, receiving them with less resistance (Logel and Cohen, 2012).

4. They make us less likely to dismiss harmful health messages, instead responding with the intention to change for the better (Harris et al., 2007), including eating more fruit and vegetables (Epton and Harris, 2008).

5. They have been linked positively to academic achievement, mitigating GPA decline in students who feel "left out" at college (Layous et al., 2017).

6. Self-affirmation lowers stress and rumination (Koole et al., 1999; Weisenfeld et al., 2001).[3]

Declare and decree your way out!

From a Christian perspective, we can apply this practice with biblically-based affirmations we speak to ourselves, known as declarations or decrees. In this, we reaffirm to ourselves who God says we are and His promises to us, which are yes and amen in Christ (2 Cor. 1:20). How absolutely awesome it is to realize the power and authority we access as heirs of God the Father and joint heirs with Christ Jesus the Son. There are countless examples of this principle documented in the Word of God, two of which are found in Mark 11:23 and Matthew 18:18:

> For assuredly, I say to you, whoever says to this mountain, "Be removed and be cast into the sea," and does not doubt in his heart, but believes that those things he says will be done, he will have whatever he says.
> —Mark 11:23

> Truly I tell you, whatever you bind on earth, will be bound in heaven, and whatever you loose on earth will be loosed in heaven.
> —Matthew 18:18, niv

Within these two scriptures alone rest endless possibilities to decree and declare manifested change over our current situation. Many times, we find ourselves using the words "decree" and "declare" synonymously; and although they can be used in conjunction with each other, I believe they are not the same. A spiritual decree is defined as a rule, law, promise, or principle issued by someone in high authority (God) operating on behalf of said authority.

In contrast, a spiritual declaration is "a formal, verbal or written, expression of allegiance to, or alliance with, a specific decree already established." Therefore, God, having all power and authority, issued certain decrees in His Word. We, being His heirs and kingdom citizens, can, by virtue of our relationship with Him, declare with certainty by faith, our allegiance and agreement in regard to these decrees. Once we begin to realize the power of His Word released into the atmosphere through what we speak and declare, our language changes, and so too, will our perception, and ultimately, our situation.

One of the affirmations—my "I am" statements—I use daily is "I am healthy, physically fit, spiritually emotionally, and intellectually equipped." I base it on 3 John 1:2: "Beloved, I pray that you may prosper in all things and be in health, just as your soul prospers."

Joel Osteen has a book called *The Power of I Am*, in which he teaches the value of declaring who we are based on Bible principles. His book is one of my go-tos when I am in my car. It gives me positive energy and the opportunity to practice consistency with my positive affirmations.[4]

Leaders who use affirmations or declarations are much more successful in the long run. The main thing is to ensure you are changing the negative self-talk that might be going on in your head. You are a constant thinker. Ensuring those thoughts and the things you say to yourself are positive and spiritually enriching is critical. Therefore, make sure the declarations, affirmations, and "I am" statements you use are biblically based. For example, you can say, "I am fearfully and wonderfully made," even if you don't feel so wonderful in the moment. When you recite positive and godly messages over and over, they help to override the negative thoughts, replacing them with positive, godly content.

You can use books like *The Power of I Am* to learn declarations that have already been authored or you can develop some of your own based on your favorite scriptures or biblical principles. If you choose to develop your own, make them short and specific to the situation at hand. Memorize scriptures to combat your negative thinking. I have provided some starter affirmations with scriptures for you in appendix C: Thirty-One Days of Eikonic Prayers and Declarations. It's best to utilize these affirmations early in the morning to start your day. (See Mark 1:35.)

3. SET BOUNDARIES

Setting boundaries is a healthy practice that reinforces your confidence in who you are and Who you serve. Without boundaries, you easily fall victim to exploitation, aimless wandering, and feeling out of place. The Bible says a city without walls, or boundaries, is susceptible to infiltration and attack. When you lack boundaries, it is as if you have no control over what God has put within your realm to manage and steward, and this includes yourself and your gifts. (See Proverbs 25:28.) Without boundaries, you will surely fall prey to the nine spirits I listed in chapter two.

Essentially, a boundary is "a line that marks the limits of an area; a dividing line."[5] It is a border, frontier, partition, divider, line, cutoff point, or threshold. A boundary basically states, "This stops here." Dr. Henry Cloud, author of the bestselling book, *Boundaries for Leaders*, says, "You are always going to get a combination of two things: what you create and what you allow."[6] Set boundaries for yourself and for others to help you remain at peak performance.

Setting boundaries for yourself—accountability

To keep yourself in check, you need a person to whom you can be accountable. This person cannot be intimidated by you and must be able to speak the truth to you in love. This person also must be someone you respect—someone to whom you will listen, someone you take seriously, and someone you cannot manipulate using your intellect and negotiation skills. Ideally, this person has a strong prayer life and is prophetically gifted. They must be able to petition heaven on your behalf and help you through to your healing, deliverance, and restoration when you need it.

Before being accountable to another human, you need to be accountable to God. How is your prayer life? As I have said before, consider King David, a classic example of one who knew how to go to the throne room with everything laid out before God. He was honest and open to the leading and correction of God. You must create a lifeline to God through prayer, Bible study, worship, and fellowship with His people.

You need this to keep yourself submitted to following God's plans for your life.

Setting boundaries for others—let loyalty decide

Another way you can nurture and guard your creative genius is to choose your relationships wisely. Be attentive to who wants to be attached to you. There may have been times throughout your journey when you allowed naysayers, destiny hijackers, dream killers, false spiritual leaders, and purpose thieves to infuse doubt and insecurity into your life. This may have caused you to abort your assignment or made you feel unqualified to activate your gifts or follow through to finish anything. This will not do. These types of individuals cannot go to the next level with you. You must set boundaries to ensure your inner circle—your accountability circle, your tribe—is loyal, truth-telling, loving, and respectful. Boundaries can be loosened when it comes to those you serve, but not with those with whom you are aligned. Just as you support and champion them, they must be ready to stand with you when stuff hits the fan and restore you when you're broken.

To help you know what to look for, Dr. Matthew Stevenson, author and pastor of All Nations Worship Assembly, gives these five signs of healthy loyalty:

1. Consistent communication—There is a dialect established in every relationship consisting of key terms, phrases, and meanings which uphold the strength of the relationship. The time margins of this vary, relationship to relationship, but loyalty is generally not silent.

2. Integral communication—Loyalty is an action, an attitude, and a behavior, and all of these are communication methods. Loyalty does not initiate, entertain, or involve itself in any communication, activity, or scenario that harms the relationship or counterparty. This is especially true with derogatory discussion and defamation of character.

3. Clear communication—At the point that loyalty is questioned, the relationship must be reexamined. Loyalty is not effective when it's hidden or silent. Therefore, loyalty has no problem being regularly expressive to the relationship it values. If there is no true value to the relationship, a disloyal person won't see the need to uphold or vocalize their loyalty. You should never have blurred lines when examining who is in your corner. When a person prefers ambiguous discussion about loyalty, they leave room for future betrayal.

4. Honest communication—In relationships, every action is communication. Loyalty is a character trait that mainly communicates value and protection for a relationship. If there is deception, dualism, hypocrisy, vague action, secret discussion, conspiratorial behavior, or a loss of transparency, loyalty has been damaged.

5. Upgraded communication—Loyalty evolves and matures as the relationship does. A willingness to be more loyal is necessary for any functional relationship. This requires open assessment

about breaches in trust, areas of suspicion, areas of inconsistency, and abused definitions. When a person values a relationship, they will adjust as many times as need be, without becoming self-abusive, to nurture the relationship and protect its purpose. If a person is unwilling to change for loyalty's sake, that person is loyal to nothing but themselves.[7]

If someone in your circle isn't consistently operating from a place of loyalty, it may be time to reevaluate the relationship. If you find you are not returning this level of loyalty to your spouse, business partners, or inner circle, do some self-correction. The measure in which we give out is the measure in which we receive. (See Luke 6:38.)

> You are not really a loyalist until you have walked with someone at their lowest, looked directly at their mess, and proclaimed, "I love you and I still got you!" Now, we rock with people based on their following not out of simply being faithful![8]

4. Care

Eikonic leaders are in high demand in the marketplace and ministry. We constantly provide oxygen to our staff and associates, and we forget to provide that same care to ourselves. We regularly find ourselves working long hours and consecutive days because we try to get the never-ending work completed.

We are exhausted but we feel the work will not get done if we don't keep going. Sixty-plus hour workweeks can really work against us, causing physical and emotional pain. While we are working, we are not engaged in productive relationships that can refuel us.

When was the last time you felt rested and not overworked? When did you last resuscitate yourself or give yourself AIR or an oxygen mask? If it's been a long time, so long you can't recall, you are neglecting yourself and headed straight for burnout or a blow-up. You must take care of yourself to excel and thrive. Rest is a gift and a blessing from God for which you are eligible.

What I propose is that, to continue propelling forward in your iconic excellence, you need to build a regular practice of self-care into your routine. Self-care is about developing the practice of listening to your mind, body, and spirit...and doing what they say.

Here are some things you can do to properly care for yourself:

Take a vacation and enjoy some down time.

While you're in the space of self-care and rejuvenation, turn off your cell phone and take some real time for you.

If you need help, ask for it.

There is nothing wrong with asking for help when you need it, whether from a trusted friend, pastor, leader or even a mental health provider. Counseling is usually not the first option leaders consider; however, it can be a critical resource. As you know, lately, there have been a number of leaders who, in a space of hopelessness, have ended their lives. Old-school thinking has taught us we should not share our hurts and habits. With this system of belief, they may have felt as though there was no other way for them, but hear me: there is a way out.

Jesus created mental health counselors and spiritual advisors who utilize biblical answers to help others get out of life's touchiest situations. Please don't be ashamed to call upon one and seek counsel as needed.

Say no.

No is a complete sentence and one of the most powerful statements we can utter. For women, in particular, this can be one of the most difficult words to say. Even when we know in our hearts no is the correct response, our inclination too often is to say yes to please someone else and to be perceived as nice or likable. It just seems so much easier—and less confrontational—to say yes. If we somehow find the courage to say no, it is often saturated by a sweet, syrupy, long, drawn-out explanation to cover our guilt and perhaps still allow us to be seen favorably in someone else's eyes. But there is very real harm that can come from not saying a firm and confident no.

No is a boundary word. When we can't establish our no, we end up doing things that aren't assigned to us and suffering all sorts of issues stemming from not knowing who we are. You've come so far and sacrificed so much. Don't let fear of no and fear of man sabotage all of that for you.

There is a rich story in the Word about a time when Jesus had to tell two people whom He loved dearly that He wasn't going to come when they needed Him. (See John 11:1–44.) Martha, who served Jesus, and Mary, the very one who poured perfumed oil on His feet and washed them with her hair, sent word their brother, Lazarus, Jesus's beloved, was sick and needed Him to come right away to see about him. Jesus's response? No. He said it seemingly with no explanation...and Lazarus died. Selah. Ultimately, Jesus remained focused on the activities which brought God glory, not those which would have made others happy. This should be your primary focus as well.

Be proactive in your communication and ask for what you need.

As an iconic leader, I have often been told others don't know what I want. I find that interesting because I am very direct. What I have learned is I sometimes assume people should be able to read my thoughts and know my needs. One of my previous pastors, Keith Graham, said you have to tell people what you need and want. Iconic leader, you can't put the burden of knowing what you want on people nor assume they can read your mind or know your thoughts and expectations. If you want to have successful interactions with others, communicate your needs clearly, telling them what you need from them. This way, they know how to communicate with you and give you what you need from them. They will not be forced to assume and run the risk of getting things wrong, creating additional stress and frustration and later wasting time redoing what could have been done right the first time. Let your yeas be yeas and your nays be nays (Matt. 5:37).

GIVE YOURSELF AIR

Believe it or not, the four actions we discuss in this chapter are much like your self-prescribed AIR process. By embracing and affirming your identity in Christ, and by setting boundaries and caring for yourself, you self-*activate*, self-*impart*, and self-*release* as God gives His divine wisdom for you to do so.

YOUR OXYGEN MASK

1. Are you living an authentic life? What behaviors that you practice indicate that you embrace your whole, authentic self?

2. Do you honor loyalty? Do you practice loyalty, giving it equally as you expect to receive it?

3. When was the last time you said no when you were tempted to say yes? What was the outcome of saying no and how did it make you feel? Similarly, when was the last time you said yes when you wanted to and knew you should have said no? How did saying yes impact you, positively or negatively?

4. Do you practice affirmations or some other form of self-care? Is it a regular part of your routine? If you don't but would like to, what is a first step you are willing to take and easily incorporate into your routine?

Chapter 8

LEADING THE NEXT ICONIC GENERATION

Though each iconic leader is distinct, they have the unmatched ability to raise up and mentor other iconic leaders and leave a meaningful legacy in their wake. In the next few pages, I will help you discover how you can harness the seven strengths unique to the iconic leader as mentor and add AIR to your mentoring process.

Leaders are important in all facets of our lives. Whether it is at work, home, church, or play, a defined leadership structure is critical to functionality and success. Leaders have been with us from the beginning of time, and the idea that as human beings we need a leader is not based on societal rules nor because someone in authority says so. In fact, the need for leadership is inherent in and represents a natural human instinct. This desire to be led is true even among those who are in leadership positions. There are leaders, and then there are leaders of leaders.

Throughout our history, we have seen leaders rise and fall. There have been those who left an indelible mark on society because of their exemplary leadership skills. These are the leaders we seek to emulate. As Christians, we know the ultimate leader is God, and accordingly, we all answer to His higher authority. However, as we canvas and study the great world leaders of our time, we can understand the nature of leadership, and more importantly, emulate their best practices and behaviors to become the balanced and effective iconic leaders we aim to be with character traits we can proudly pass on to those we mentor.

Seven Strengths of an Iconic Leader Mentor

As a professional coach and consultant in the field of leadership, I come across many individuals who are looking for a mentor. So the need for mentorship is great—we know this. However, being a great mentor is what we aim for so we can see a new generation of iconic leaders soar past the hardships and hindrances that may have stalled us in various seasons.

As an iconic leader, you, within your own right, are superb at what you do. You generally strive for excellence and are gifted in your area of specialization. Accordingly, you will make a great mentor. To give you some points to aim for as you help to raise up the next generation of iconic leaders, here are seven strengths you need to infuse in all of your mentorship relationships.

1. The iconic leader mentor challenges your thinking.

Whether you work in corporate America or are walking in your purpose as a ministry leader, critical thinking is paramount for success. Conversations with your mentee should challenge them and push them to be better. Get them thinking outside of the box. Give them suggestions and advice that keeps them up at night.

You may find having some of these more challenging conversations is not easy and your mentee may repel them at first but help them to know that, if they are to get to the next level in their career, business, or ministry, they must leave their comfort zone.

2. The iconic leader mentor is not afraid to upset you.

The mentoring relationship is a two-way street producing benefits for both the mentor and the mentee. However, your mentee has more to lose if the mentorship is dissolved. Accordingly, you cannot sugar-coat information and circumstances to make the steps toward progression and promotion seem easy. If your intention is to help your mentee meet their objectives, you need to be the iconic mentor who will never be afraid of upsetting them.

You understand that higher expectations reap higher rewards. So, let them get upset. At times, they may get on your nerves, and there may be days when they are frustrated with you and the process. Be unapologetic about pushing them even when it gets them upset. You will earn their respect and gratitude.

3. The iconic leader mentor demands excellence.

Excellence looks different for everyone. Your higher standard of excellence will attract the right mentee who is seeking to grow—for real. The end objective of mentoring is not for lateral movement but to move upward in a specific field or ministry, increasing results and influence. As an iconic leader, you have the mindset and life experience that will demand a certain level of excellence relevant to your mentee's profession, business, or ministry.

4. The iconic leader mentor has great character.

A mentee needs a mentor with impeccable character whose integrity and ethics are above reproach. Iconic leaders fit this criterion well. You have a track record of excellence and a moral code such that others easily speak well of you. This will be a deciding factor for your mentee as they select the right mentor. This also means what you pass on to them will be balanced, righteous, and eternal.

5. The iconic leader mentor is a model in your area of focus.

Mentors must teach by example. They help a mentee grow in their field. That growth may include advancing in their career, opening a profitable business, or developing spiritually in ministry work. You ought to be a model of what the mentee hopes to achieve. Be transparent and open so they see the struggle and can watch you overcome. By your example, they will become fit to excel in the field in which they serve.

6. The iconic leader mentor believes in your potential.

Mentors prefer to work with individuals who show potential. Believing in your mentee's potential is key to having the passion to invest in their success. If you don't see nor believe in their potential, your work with them may be a waste of time. Accordingly, you will believe in the skills, talent, and gifts of your mentee. You know that with your tools and strategies, they will be successful in their endeavors.

In your own mentor relationship, be aware that not all mentors are interested in your progress. You want to stay away from mentors who are focused on self-gain. The iconic leader mentor will value your gifts and bring out the best in you.

7. The iconic leader mentor is a great listener.

The ideal mentor should not be a perpetual talker who fails to listen to concerns or the mentee's desires. As an iconic leader mentor, you must be a great listener, able to hear not just what your mentee is saying but also what they don't say, affording them the opportunity to engage in conversation in a meaningful and successful way.

Remember, mentoring is a two-way, beneficial learning opportunity in which you share advice, knowledge, and experience to take your mentee from where they are now to where they want to be or beyond. The signs I shared above will help you serve as the right kind of iconic leader mentor and even to select the right mentor for yourself.

Add AIR to Your Mentoring Process

One of the themes I have been repeating throughout this book is the need to breathe spiritual oxygen and AIR—activate, impart, and release—into your work or ministry as an iconic leader. Spiritual oxygen has everything to do with how you flow with the Spirit of God, knowing His heartbeat for you and those you serve and sensing where the wind of His Spirit is flowing so that you are always in the right place at the right time with the right people doing the right thing. You can infuse your daily life with spiritual oxygen by continuing to apply the principles and strategies we've discussed in previous chapters.

AIR is the outward-facing or actionable part of this concept. AIR is about how others invest in you and how you invest in others. It houses three important actions in your relationships with other leaders as you are mentored, counseled, and launched forward. They are also important as you reach back into your sphere of influence and answer the call to raise up other iconic leaders.

The three parts of AIR in motion look like this:

1. Activate—Identify strengths and weaknesses and affirm your mentee's iconic identity. You may invite them to work through this book with you and to take the Eikonic Leader Assessment in appendix A. As you and your mentee work together to discover their unique iconic makeup, you will find ways to stretch them in their talents and abilities and to teach/mentor them by providing feedback.

2. Impart—Most of the time your mentee can't see how they are able to do what is required of them because they've been on their own for some time. Your role is to coach them along until they are comfortable. Continue to provide feedback and model for them the behaviors and actions you advise as they begin to move forward.

3. Release—Once you and your mentee feel comfortable, find ways to begin to release them into destiny, purpose, and assignment. You may have colleagues or minister friends who need a good leader on their team. Refer your mentee to them with your recommendation. You can also challenge your mentee to ask for more responsibility in the place where they currently work or serve. Then, stick by them through the transition.

We breathe AIR into others' destinies when we challenge them, share wisdom, open doors, and cheer them on. Success is a collaborative effort. No one gets to the mountaintop alone. As you seek to push others forward through mentoring and in line with God's leading, you will want to have that alone time with Him we discussed in chapter four under "When It's OK to Go Alone," and in chapter seven, where we discussed being accountable to Him. As a leader, you must hear from God. Fast, pray, and get to a place of inspiration when you need wisdom on how to influence others righteously. We truly do our best in community, and your leadership style poured out on others is integral to the community's thriving.

How I Give AIR

As I have said, I have mentored, counseled, and consulted with individuals and organizations over the years and have leveraged my iconic identity to help them rise to a whole new level. In the process, I defined how I would give AIR to them to see them achieve their objective. The results have been phenomenal.

My way of giving AIR looks like this:

I know the perfect balance between work and play.

I incorporate laughing, joking, and connecting with those I lead to let them see that excelling in your gift, calling, or assignment is invigorating and fun. When you operate at the center of who you are with people who value you, the line between work and play can become so fine it is hard to tell which you are doing.

I turn correcting mistakes into encouragement and valuable lessons.

We all make mistakes, and while they can set projects or timelines back, they happen. There is never a need to belittle or berate the person who made the mistake. It is my goal to never make anyone feel stupid about the mistake they've made. Rather, I try to ask questions to help them analyze how they could have handled the situation differently. I actively listen for their answer and give guiding feedback. No one "gets away" with anything and I don't enable bad behavior, but I empower them to be responsible for their successes and failures.

I address misunderstandings head on.

If there's ever a misunderstanding among those I lead or even between them and me, I initiate a forum for a discussion. Constructive, solution-oriented communication is so important to keep the air clear and for good work to continue. I don't waste time. The longer a leader waits to address situations like this, the more likely problems will fester and transform into big dramatic situations that could have been avoided. I value the ones God has assigned to me too much to let us be taken out by something so easily avoided. I make it a point to be transparent and direct, so my mentees and other leaders with whom I serve are able to give that back to me.

I don't let anyone get too comfortable.

Greatness is in each one of us. If there is no one to push you into beginning that new assignment, making that move across the country, or starting that business, how will you feel the boldness to do it? All it takes is one trustworthy person to say, "Yes, you can do it. You have what it takes. This is your time. Go for it." When I see potential in those around me, I push them toward their next.

An Iconic Future

God is doing a new thing in the earth and iconic leaders are on the front lines of this epic happening. As we keep ourselves healthy, balanced, and in tune with the Spirit of God, He will continue to fortify us with the strength of character, excellence, integrity, insight, vision, and drive that He has placed in each of us.

We are hard-wired to be ideal partners with Him as He expands His kingdom. We are bold and brave enough reach back to systems that still work while reaching forward in to the promising abyss of the unknown and chart new paths. Once we come out of our think tanks and cognitive caves, we have the confidence and wisdom to reach out to our tribe and pull together strategies that help propel our mission into the future.

What we have experienced until now is the breaking of old systems and traditions of men that don't work. We have felt the constricting pull of the status quo and the resistance of those who fear the loss of their power and influence. But regardless of what old things some want to hold on to, things are changing. God says, "Behold, I will do a new thing, now it shall spring forth; shall you not know it?"

The iconic leader in you answers back, "Yes, God I see it and I know it."

You hear the cry of the earth groaning for the sons and daughters of God to arise (Rom. 8:19). You know that what no longer works for the future of what God has planned must be uprooted while what will help it manifest must be planted and cultivated. You sense the changing of the guard and a passing of the baton and know that the transition is inevitable.

Your challenge is to submit to God and those with whom He is aligning you with so that you will have the help and support you need to bring forward His plans and destiny for your life. You must be mentored and, as you are supported in that way, you must reach out to mentor the next generation of iconic leaders. This is how each generation gets what it needs to carry out God's plans.

With the dawn of leaders such as Steve Jobs of Apple, Jeff Bezos of Amazon, Mark Zuckerberg of Facebook, Susan Wojciki of Youtube, Barak Obama, Michelle Obama, Ava Duvernay, Oprah Winfrey, Angela Merkel, chancellor of Germany, and so many others who break the mold, social systems

Leading the Next Eikonic Generation

are being forced to make room for a more idea-driven and creative style of leadership. This glimpse of the future of leadership is proving that iconic leadership is becoming more in demand.

Are you ready to go from unnoticed, untolerated, and overlooked to recognized, celebrated, and overbooked? Your brand of creativity and insight coupled with a drive to follow through no matter the cost is what our times demand. Our culture has made the shift from a religious, rigid, and traditional generation to a generation that craves authenticity, transparency, and relationship. The iconic leader is already there; everyone else is still catching up.

My prayer for you is that you have been encouraged and strengthened as you were presented a new way to see yourself in these pages. Hold this book close as God takes you from glory to glory and faith to faith. You have no ceiling, but wait on God. He will elevate you at the right time. He will help you flourish in your fit. You will have the needed solitude to produce excellence. You will also find a community in which you can be your true self.

My challenge for you as you go on from here is to guard your heart (Prov. 4:23) and keep it pure and clean before God. Keep Psalm 51:10—"Create in me a clean heart, O God, and renew a steadfast spirit within me"—close to your heart as life pushes against your unique light. You want to keep your heart in this place because everything you put out—multiply, give, and reproduce—must represent your Creator if it is to have any real value or lasting effect.

You are iconic. Never doubt your value or how much you are needed to be your full and authentic self.

Your Oxygen Mask

1. Have you found the right iconic leader mentor for you? Do you have a mentor? If you have a mentor but feel they are not the right mentor, what is lacking in your mentor relationship?

2. Which of the seven strengths of an iconic leader mentor are most important to you, and why?

3. Are you serving as an iconic leader mentor? Do you embody the seven strengths of an iconic leader mentor? Which, if any, of the seven strengths are a challenge for you, and what steps can you take to embody and display more of this strength as you mentor others?

Appendix A

THE EIKONIC LEADER ASSESSMENT

Have you ever tried to figure out just which type of leader you are? You go online and complete a bunch of personality tests which leave you even more confused. As I noted earlier, chances are you just don't fit into any one box. The dynamics of your personality and leadership style are unique and multidimensional.

I know this feeling too well. I am that misunderstood leader who oftentimes sticks out in a crowd of other leaders. Because you don't fit into the box created by the majority, you are in a class by yourself. It is time to embrace who you really are! There is a name for this type of leader. You are an iconic leader and you are not the only one.

After working with leaders and leaders of leaders for years, I have noticed many of them have never completed a personality test. While personality tests do not provide the answer to how you should lead, personality tests or similarly, leadership style tests, are a great way to better understand who you are and how to use your leadership qualities to maximize results.

To help you identify the level at which you display iconic

leader traits, I developed this assessment. There are three levels I defined for this assessment:

1. The iconic leader in the making

2. The ideal iconic leader

3. The extreme iconic leader

You can fill out the relevant table on the pages of this book or record your answers in your journal or on a separate sheet of paper. There are no right or wrong answers to this test. The objective is to identify traits in your personality that help to confirm the level of iconic leader you are. All you need to do is be honest in your self-assessment. Use the numbers 0, 1, 2, or 3 to score yourself for each trait.

The Assessment

For each answer:

- 0 = Never; I cannot relate to this personality trait at all.

- 1 = Rarely; there have been a few isolated situations where this trait shines through.

- 2 = Sometimes; I identify with this personality trait, but it is a reflection of who I am less than most of the time.

The Eikonic Leader Assessment

- 3 = Always; the statement is a reflection of who I am most, if not all, of the time.

	Personality Traits	**Score**
1	I consider myself to be an individualist. I understand teamwork, but I prefer to work alone.	
2	I am concerned others may not get the same results that I will. Therefore, I prefer to do the work myself.	
3	I am multitalented and possess a number of gifts.	
4	I know what I am capable of achieving, and I am OK with keeping it to myself.	
5	People think I am a jack-of-all-trades, but in reality, I master everything I do.	
6	I live in a state of excellence, and anything less than that is not acceptable for me.	
7	People think I am a perfectionist, but if perfection equals excellence, then I am a perfectionist.	
8	When it comes to service to others, I operate in excellence even if it is not for profit.	
9	I have been called arrogant and sometimes even cocky.	
10	People just don't get me. They think I am a "know it all" with a bad attitude.	

11	I don't like passive aggressive behavior. I prefer direct communication.	
12	People get offended because I generally get right to the point and don't beat around the bush.	
13	I am a big-picture person. I leave the finer details to someone else.	
14	I need highly stimulating conversation. I get bored with meaningless fluff and gimmicks.	
15	I maintain few but very meaningful and long-standing friendships	

The Results

The personality traits listed in the table represent characteristics of the iconic leader. Now that you have completed your assessment, let's look at the results. If you answered as truthfully as you could, you should be able to see clearly where you stand. If you had some difficulty knowing your inclinations, it may be a good idea to get feedback from someone who is close to you.

Once you feel you have landed at the right responses, tally all the answers. The sum will represent your test score. Note your score cannot exceed 45. Your total represents where you fall on the iconic leader spectrum.

0–15: The iconic leader in the making

If you score anywhere from 0 to 15 on the test, you possess few of the qualities of the iconic leader. And if you desire to pursue the full identity, you represent the iconic leader in the making yet, at present, your personality traits are at the lower end of the spectrum.

Since you only possess few characteristics of the iconic leader, it is easy for you to blend in and incorporate other leadership styles to achieve your goals. If you fall in this group, it is easy for you to play down your iconic leadership traits. However, if you can embrace and learn how to use these traits, you will quickly realize iconic results in your leadership positions.

16–30: The ideal iconic leader

A score from 16 to 30 represents the center of the spectrum, and you are the ideal iconic leader. You possess the traits that are easily misunderstood, especially as a leader. However, you own the ideal blend of characteristics of the iconic leader and are excellent in all you do. You may find it hard to fit in, but you do not see that as a negative. You are OK with not being the average leader. You are an iconic leader.

31–45: The extreme iconic leader

You are the leader of all leaders and represent the highest level on the spectrum. You have led your life believing you should change and are always misunderstood by those around you.

Managing your extreme personality characteristics can be very difficult, especially among those who do not understand your bluntness and strive for excellence. However, there is no hiding your iconic leadership qualities. In fact, your presence exudes leadership and people who follow or lead alongside you either hate you or love you. Your leadership qualities may seem like a curse, but when you learn how to manage them to generate results, you will quickly begin to embrace the iconic leader in you.

Understanding the Qualities of the Iconic Leader

Armed with your score and information as to where you fall on the spectrum of iconic leadership, refer back to chapter one of this book for an overall picture of who you are as an iconic leader. For a direct connection to this assessment, there are five main signs of iconic leadership I'd like to highlight.

Individualism—alone in the crowd

As I mentioned in chapter 3, the iconic leader understands the team dynamic and enjoys working with a great, motivated group. However, the iconic leader often finds themselves alone in their high levels of intensity, urgency, and excellence. When this is the case, the iconic leader would much rather work alone. If you indicated an always or sometimes for question 1, 2, and 15 in the test, you are the iconic leader who will work alone if there are no other like-minded teammates to help produce the desired results.

Multiple gifts and talents

The iconic leader possesses several layers of gifts and talents but prefers not to draw too much attention to how gifted they are. They are multidimensional. This leader is good at a few things and master of none. No way! The iconic leader masters almost everything he or she puts their hands to and performs those tasks with excellence. Because of this, the iconic leader finds it hard to choose any one thing to focus on.

Unfortunately, many iconic leaders will try to choose just one thing to focus on because that's what the world dictates. They cannot choose any one thing and as a result, end up doing nothing at all. As an iconic leader, you are not wired to be either/or. You can be both/and. The iconic leader has the ability to be multifaceted is not arrogant and pompous. In fact, they are reluctant to let others know about the multitude of gifts they possess. If you answered in the affirmative for question 3, 4, and 5 in the test, you possess this iconic leader characteristic.

High standard of excellence

The iconic leader has an extremely high standard of excellence, especially in relation to areas of service. The word *excellence* is often used by leaders to explain the results needed, even required, from those they lead. For the iconic leader, excellence is not a request; it is a way of life.

As an iconic leader, you live in a state of excellence and expect the same from others, but the excellence required by you is not that which will lead to average or standard results. As an iconic leader, I am sure you get annoyed when others claim to operate in a standard of excellence yet their mode of operation and/or their results are far removed from what you expect. The iconic leader demands an extremely high standard of excellence.

This characteristic is particularly important when carrying out acts or projects in the areas of service. Even if the work is voluntary, the standard of excellence required by the iconic leader is as high as in work for profit.

For my standard, I vowed to do my best to operate in the spirit of excellence in everything I do. I set the bar myself. For entrepreneurs, it's having a strong brand identity. For ministries, it's having the right people in place who can help you build your vision of excellence. In mentorship, it's ensuring you have someone who understands leadership and who sometimes brings correction to your life.

If you are an entrepreneur, visionary, or pastor, having people of excellence with these qualities is essential to doing things in excellence. Questions 6, 7, 8, and 14 in the test relates to this quality of an iconic leader.

Misunderstood personality

From chapter 3, we learned the iconic leader's multiple talents and high standard of excellence often lead to being misunderstood and mistaken for arrogant and cocky, they are often viewed as complex. Test questions 9, 10, and 13 deals with this trait.

Direct personality

The iconic leader is very direct and to the point and is sometimes outspoken and seen to be abrasive though personal offense is not intended. Questions 11 and 12 in the test relate to this leadership quality.

Now That You Know— What's Next?

For years, you may have been walking around thinking something was wrong with you and that you needed to change. However, we are not the same as others. Indeed, we are made differently, and it is time for you to embrace the iconic leader in you.

Now that you know who you are, you realize the problem lies not in you, but in others who are unable to understand your worth. You have many gifts and talents you need to use. It is sad to see so much potential and so many gifts go unused and unnoticed, because church decision-makers or corporate America's leaders don't know what to do with you. When you submit to God and walk in purpose, you will lose the need to be understood.

Iconic leaders lead with intentionality. Iconic leaders are focused on the lives they touch and deposit into. We must be cognizant of the great mandate we carry and are assigned to. This requires looking at ourselves and breathing life into others.

You are who you are because God intends to use you to bring about change and transformation. You bear His image and you are charged with bringing His glory to the four corners of the Earth. Apologize no longer for your quirks and idiosyncrasies. Come under the authority of the Spirit of God and walk confidently in the excellence bestowed upon you.

You have purpose and a destiny you cannot afford to hide. Come out from where you are, forgive others and yourself, align with the right people, and do what God has sent you to do. You are iconic, and the world needs you.

Appendix B

THE EIKONIC LEADER SOUL-CARE ASSESSMENT

IT IS NO surprise, with all the complexity, talent, and skill inherent in iconic leaders, many carry heavy burdens of responsibility. Over time and without the proper support system, this type of leader can begin to buckle. Moreover, because of the brute strength central to this leadership style, the signs of a impending breakdown may be overlooked or ignored.

In order for you to operate at a continuously high standard and to produce the level of works that brings fulfillment, you must stay connected to your inner self. You may even have come into this journey already feeling depleted and out of energy, or you may sense what you've been called to do requires you to remain filled inside if you are to serve and give and make the difference you desire to make.

With this in mind, I have designed this sixteen-statement Eikonic Leader Soul-Care Assessment to help you examine the state of your soul as a person in a leadership role, within ministry or marketplace. Depending on how you respond, this assessment will let you know whether you are leading out of exhaustion and your soul needs some care or you are thriving. This assessment digs deep into your thoughts and into your emotional process. It touches on your energy, character, and creativity and will allow you to assess your mental and emotional status so that you do not fall into the cycle of leading out of robotics or numbness. You don't want to ever hide the state where you really are emotionally, spiritually, or mentally. Don't follow the poor habits of some leaders who've gone before you by not being transparent and ignoring symptoms of burnout and exhaustion. This assessment will help you know if you need to take a breath of fresh air and reenergize and refresh yourself so you can continue to function at your iconic best.

As you take the assessment, prayerfully reflect on each statement. Ask God to help you see the state of your heart and soul for where they truly are. Do this for each statement as you approach it. Then choose the option on the scale that represents where you are. I ask that you do this as honestly as you can.

These questions are not meant to produce guilt, shame, or a sense of failure. Rather, they are intended to help you to be honest with yourself and the state of your soul. This assessment digs deep into your thoughts and emotional processes and touches on your energy, character, and creativity. Truthfully examining these aspects of you will allow you to assess your mental and emotional state. Most leaders continue to lead from a place of exhaustion, stress, and being overwhelmed, and eventually become numb to the passion and dreams they once held. They are not transparent with those in their inner circle. They ignore symptoms of the need to take a breath of fresh air and reenergize or refresh themselves, so they can be effective in order to reach their goals. By God's grace, this will not be your story.

This is a first step toward ensuring you find rather than lose your soul in the context of your ministry or workplace leadership. Your wholeness is imperative for growth.

If, while completing this soul-care assessment, you begin to feel overwhelmed, please stop. Circle the number for the statement or statements that caused the overwhelm. Step away and take some time to reflect on your feelings and what part of the statement took you to that place. You may even need to get your journal and write out what just happened.

When you are able, please come back to where you left off and complete the rest of the assessment, rating each item accordingly on the presented scale.

This assessment covers many of the common leadership symptoms of fatigue and the many thoughts and emotions that arise to alert you that you are at that breaking point. Not meant to be a stand-alone diagnostic tool, this assessment can be helpful in indicating the presence and degree of where you are.

The Assessment

Using the scale below as your guide, mark on a separate sheet of paper or circle right here on the pages of your book the appropriate response number to each statement below. Once you have answered all of the questions, you will be instructed on how to calculate your score to get your results.

Rating scale

0	Never / rarely
1	Occasionally / Slightly
2	Moderate in intensity or frequency
3	Intense / severe or frequent

• • •

1. More and more I am feeling empty and disconnected, like I am watching a movie and I am the lead actor in it. I am not experiencing the pleasures of life, and I am manufacturing emotions that are not a true reflection of how I really feel. I am not enjoying the service or ministry I provide to others in this season as I once did.

   0 – Never/rarely

   1 – Occasionally/slightly

   2 – Moderate in intensity or frequency

   3 – Intense/severe or frequent

2. I have a nagging feeling of spiritual emptiness, like I'm not being fulfilled in my daily marketplace or ministry job. I know something doesn't seem quite normal, but I don't know how to make the connection or even figure it out. It's a feeling like nobody even cares.

The Eikonic Leader Soul-Care Assessment

0 – Never/rarely

1 – Occasionally/slightly

2 – Moderate in intensity or frequency

3 – Intense/severe or frequent

3. My life is so hectic. I have multiple things to do and don't feel as if I am resolving or accomplishing any of them. I feel as if I am running in circles and nothing is moving. I feel like I am stagnant, like a hamster on a wheel—moving but going nowhere.

0 – Never/rarely

1 – Occasionally/slightly

2 – Moderate in intensity or frequency

3 – Intense/severe or frequent

4. I am going through the motions of my daily tasks every day, whether it's ministry within the marketplace or management. I feel like I don't know who I am or where I fit within this crazy world. I am not feeling confident about where I belong or what I do well, neither am I sure what my purpose is. I feel like a failure.

0 – Never/rarely

1 – Occasionally/slightly

2 – Moderate in intensity or frequency

   3 – Intense/severe or frequent

5. Emotionally, I am tired and drained and don't feel creative or like doing anything new. I start and stop projects, and it's hard for me to complete something without extra energy given to it. Things that used to come natural and give me oxygen (energy) every day have become more like a chore. I am emotionally, spiritually, and physically drained. I don't know how to revive myself.

   0 – Never/rarely

   1 – Occasionally/slightly

   2 – Moderate in intensity or frequency

   3 – Intense/severe or frequent

6. I cannot remember things as easily as I used to. The things I did yesterday or even this week I cannot remember. I am also restless, unable to sleep at night, and irritable. It's hard for me to stay focused.

   0 – Never/rarely

   1 – Occasionally/slightly

   2 – Moderate in intensity or frequency

   3 – Intense/severe or frequent

7. I give out of my own need. I help others just to feel my self-worth, when I really don't have anything to give. My cup is empty.

   0 – Never/rarely

   1 – Occasionally/slightly

   2 – Moderate in intensity or frequency

   3 – Intense/severe or frequent

8. I don't feel any emotions right now. I don't enjoy life. I feel like I am a victim. Nothing is going my way, and I feel defeated and depleted in every area. I am emotionally numb to what is going on in my life right now.

   0 – Never/rarely

   1 – Occasionally/slightly

   2 – Moderate in intensity or frequency

   3 – Intense/severe or frequent

9. I'm constantly asking why is this happening to me? Why is my life turning out this way? I am a good person, and I will do anything for anybody but there is nobody there to be there for me. Nobody is hearing my inner cry for help. I feel exhausted.

0 – Never/rarely

1 – Occasionally/slightly

2 – Moderate in intensity or frequency

3 – Intense/severe or frequent

10. I find myself trying to find things to do, to take away the pain I feel each day. I either watch television, overeat, or daydream about living a life other than my own.

0 – Never/rarely

1 – Occasionally/slightly

2 – Moderate in intensity or frequency

3 – Intense/severe or frequent

11. I find myself not able to get organized either at home or at work. It's exhausting for me to even think about getting things together. My closets are a mess, I feel like I am hoarding things. Not sure how to start to get my life back on track. I feel unorganized.

0 – Never/rarely

1 – Occasionally/slightly

2 – Moderate in intensity or frequency

The Eikonic Leader Soul-Care Assessment

   3 – Intense/severe or frequent

12. I find myself subconsciously moving away from people because I don't trust anymore. I feel lonely and all alone. Interactions with people take whatever energy I have at the time. I can't stay focused. I don't feel like anyone even cares about my situation or circumstance.

   0 – Never/rarely

   1 – Occasionally/slightly

   2 – Moderate in intensity or frequency

   3 – Intense/severe or frequent

13. I find myself withdrawing from my spiritual life, prayer, reading the Word, and connecting with God. Things that used to provide relief for me don't do it anymore. It's become a chore to do them.

   0 – Never/rarely

   1 – Occasionally/slightly

   2 – Moderate in intensity or frequency

   3 – Intense/severe or frequent

14. I have not felt connected to the people at church or to the presence of God. I feel like my

relationship with God is fading away. After many attempts, I can't seem to find my way back to Him.

   0 – Never/rarely

   1 – Occasionally/slightly

   2 – Moderate in intensity or frequency

   3 – Intense/severe or frequent

15. I like I am good for nothing. I don't feel like I can do presentations, public speaking or stand in front of people as I used to. I don't feel like I can do what I loved to do in terms of managing people or ministering to them.

   0 – Never/rarely

   1 – Occasionally/slightly

   2 – Moderate in intensity or frequency

   3 – Intense/severe or frequent

16. I don't feel good about myself anymore. I feel like a failure and that everything I put my hands on to complete does not work out for me. My confidence is very low, and I feel depressed at times. Everything in my life seems negative.

   0 – Never/rarely

The Eikonic Leader Soul-Care Assessment

1 – Occasionally/slightly

2 – Moderate in intensity or frequency

3 – Intense/severe or frequent

The Results

Using the numbers for each response you gave above, add them all together to get a total score ranging between 0 and 48. Once you have your total score, look at the three levels that describe what your score indicates about your need for soul-care.

0–16: Personal Achievement—Thriving

You are experiencing high levels of satisfaction in ministry or marketplace and low levels of emotional exhaustion. You are thriving in your role. You feel strong, capable, competent, needed, and valued. In this season, you most likely will not need to engage in regular and frequent coaching or counseling relationship. Still, you may consider seeking professional counseling or scheduling one-on-one time with your mentor or coach when you need some objective feedback on some of the challenges you face.

17–32: Depersonalization—Happy but Exhausted

Depersonalization refers to the loss of empathy or dehumanization in interpersonal relations. A personal who displays this trait may be detached, cynical, and negative with regard to patients, clients, and colleagues. Though they generally enjoy their work and are functioning in their gifts and calling, they may feel overextended, overstimulated, and like they want to avoid social contact and withdraw.

With your results landing in this range, you may experience some of these feelings some of the time. You are what I call happy but exhausted. You are experiencing high levels of satisfaction in ministry or marketplace, but you are also experiencing higher levels of emotional exhaustion.

You will benefit from life coaching to the extent that you are willing to grow and change. You will also benefit from taking some time off for rest and recuperation. You need to unplug and be refilled for the next iconic thing you'll be assigned to do.

33–48: Burnout—Emotionally Exhausted and Unsatisfied

You are a leader in need of a sabbatical, and for too long you have been giving out of your own need. You are expressing high levels of emotional exhaustion and low levels of satisfaction and are at risk of burning out. Your feelings of personal achievement are low, and you may be dealing with excessive negative self-assessment and self-talk. You may be feeling as if the challenges you face are too difficult for you to overcome and that there is little you can do to move things forward. You may be unmotivated, feel like a failure, and doubtful of your genuine abilities to accomplish things.

If your score fell within this range, you are definitely in need of regular and intense life coaching or meeting with a licensed professional counselor. Reach out to your mentor, coach, or counselor, and schedule an appointment right away to help sort things out. You do not have to go at this alone.

The Eikonic Leader Soul-Care Assessment

If you don't have someone already designated to be there for you in this way, I want to make myself available to you. I am a certified lifestyle and leadership coach and would be happy to be of service to you wherever you are in your journey. Visit my website for more help, information, and resources: www.ansonyaburke.com.

• • •

Disclaimer: This assessment is not intended to provide a psychological or diagnosis and your completion of the test does not indicate a professional counseling or coaching relationship with the creators or administrators of this test.

Appendix C

THIRTY-ONE DAYS OF EIKONIC PRAYERS AND DECLARATIONS

A RE YOU RUNNING on empty? Feeling stuck, overwhelmed, unfulfilled, and uninspired? In desperate need of a breath of fresh AIR? These thirty-one days of iconic prayers and declarations are designed with you in mind, a leader in need of heavenly inspiration and a little room to breathe.

We constantly pour out, serve, and give of ourselves. The reality is we cannot give what we don't have. We simply cannot replenish others from an empty well. We are not called to survive; we are created to thrive.

These prayers and declarations, infused with spiritual oxygen, provide a haven from the hustle and respite for the soul. Like our bodies need oxygen, our souls need to breathe in the atmosphere of heaven. You are invited to break away from all the pressure and unending demands of leadership and, for a few precious moments, feed your spirit. Come sit at the feet of Jesus, focus on the Father, and hear what the Spirit is saying to you.

Prayer, worship, Bible study, and positive confession are

lifelines for the iconic leader. The weight of the call and responsibility to lead, mentor, motivate, and inspire require a direct connection to the heavenly stores that bring life and light to every area of life. This is why I have prepared this 31-day devotional for you.

Each daily entry is small but powerful. A Bible verse and daily declaration have been prepared for you to use as your prayer focus and intention for the day. Feel free to use these entries to jumpstart your prayer time, journaling practice, or morning routine.

You have a lot on your plate and starting your day off by engaging with the Spirit of God will fill you with what you need so you can be for others what they need. Do this with the intent to be faithful, obedient, excellent, and pleasing to the One who has given you the opportunity and capacity to do all you do.

I recommend you choose to start these prayers and declarations at the beginning of next month or at the start of a season in which you know you will need extra power. Or, of course, you can start today! Be open to what God is leading you to do.

As you inhale the supernatural power on these pages, it is my prayer you will exhale renewed vision, divine influence, and excellence for each day ahead.

Day 1

MY HEART'S DESIRE

May He grant you according to your heart's desire and fulfill all your purpose.
—Psalm 20:4

Inhale

I am highly influential. I will use my God-granted position and influence to see His Will manifested in my life and propel my purpose forward.

Exhale

What is your prayer for today? What is God saying to you?

_____

_____

_____

_____

_____

Day 2

I HAVE FAVOR

A good name is to be chosen rather than great riches, loving favor rather than silver and gold.
—Proverbs 22:1

Inhale

Heaven and Earth come into agreement with my success. I am highly sought after for my vast expertise relative to identifying the gifts and skills of those with whom I have influence.

Exhale

What is your prayer for today? What is God saying to you?

_____

_____

_____

_____

_____

_____

Eikonic Leadership

Day 3

I HAVE INFLUENCE

*A man's gift makes room for him, and
brings him before great men.*
—Proverbs 18:16

Inhale

My unique talents, abilities, and skills give me audience with influential people. God will open up avenues of divine connection and prosperity at the appointed time to fulfill His plan for ministry in my life.

Exhale

What is your prayer for today? What is God saying to you?

Eikonic Leadership

Day 4

I AM AN HEIR

And if you are Christ's, then you are Abraham's seed, and heirs according to the promise.
—Galatians 3:29

Inhale

All people relevant to the success of my business and destiny are being drawn to me today. I am a joint heir with heaven, and I claim all that is rightfully mine is coming now into my hand.

Exhale

What is your prayer for today? What is God saying to you?

Eikonic Leadership

Day 5

I AM TRUSTWORTHY

Therefore, brethren, seek out from among you seven men of good reputation, full of the Holy Spirit and wisdom, whom we may appoint over this business.
—Acts 6:3

Inhale

Leaders and peers have complete faith in me and my ability to use my giftings and skills to advance the kingdom of God.

Exhale

What is your prayer for today? What is God saying to you?

Day 6

I HAVE THE VICTORY

*But thanks be to God, who gives us the
victory through our Lord Jesus Christ.*
—1 Corinthians 15:57

Inhale

The timing of the Lord is perfect for me this day. Every minute of my day is in alignment with my victory in the marketplace.

Exhale

What is your prayer for today? What is God saying to you?

_____

_____

_____

_____

_____

_____

Day 7

I AM ACCOMPLISHED

So shall My word be that goes forth from My mouth; it shall not return to Me void, but it shall accomplish what I please, and it shall prosper in the thing for which I sent it.
—Isaiah 55:11

INHALE

I am anointed to fulfill my divine purpose and lead others to do the same. I will accomplish all He has placed in me to accomplish in business and ministry.

EXHALE

What is your prayer for today? What is God saying to you?

_____

_____

_____

_____

_____

Day 8

I HAVE THE MIND OF CHRIST

Let this mind be in you which was also in Christ Jesus.
—Philippians 2:5

Inhale

I accept the mind of Christ and declare every thought is in cooperation with God's will and destiny for my life and business.

Exhale

What is your prayer for today? What is God saying to you?

_____

_____

_____

_____

_____

_____

Eikonic Leadership

Day 9

I AM A GODLY EXAMPLE

Brethren, join in following my example, and note those who so walk, as you have us for a pattern.
—Philippians 3:17

INHALE

The strategies of heaven are being released and manifested in my life. I will rise up to lead as a godly example in my workplace.

EXHALE

What is your prayer for today? What is God saying to you?

_____

_____

_____

_____

_____

Day 10

I WALK IN LOVE

But the fruit of the Spirit is love, joy, peace, longsuffering, kindness, goodness, faithfulness, gentleness, self-control. Against such there is no law.
—Galatians 5:22–23

Inhale

I walk in love, power, and self-control. I am not influenced by emotions nor circumstances. I triumph over every plan set to ensnare me or my destiny.

Exhale

What is your prayer for today? What is God saying to you?

Day 11

I AM BOLD AND DETERMINED

*The wicked flee when no one pursues, but
the righteous are bold as a lion.*
—Proverbs 28:1

Inhale

I am bold and assertive concerning the things of God. I am completely determined to carry out His will and plan for my life and ministry.

Exhale

What is your prayer for today? What is God saying to you?

_____

_____

_____

_____

_____

_____

Day 12

I TRUST GOD

"For I know the thoughts that I think toward you," says the LORD, "thoughts of peace and not of evil, to give you a future and a hope."
—JEREMIAH 29:11

INHALE

God is shaping my circumstances and orchestrating divine appointments today for my benefit. Every day, I trust He is guiding me to fulfill His plans for my life.

EXHALE

What is your prayer for today? What is God saying to you?

_____

_____

_____

_____

_____

Eikonic Leadership

Day 13

I AM GOD'S MASTERPIECE

For we are His workmanship, created in Christ Jesus for good works, which God prepared beforehand that we should walk in them.
—Ephesians 2:10

Inhale

I am His masterpiece created for success and divinely filled to bear good and lasting fruit for the kingdom of God.

Exhale

What is your prayer for today? What is God saying to you?

_____

_____

_____

_____

_____

Eikonic Leadership

Day 14

I LIVE IN PROSPERITY

And thus you shall say to him who lives in prosperity: "Peace be to you, peace to your house, and peace to all that you have!"
—1 Samuel 25:6

Inhale

My sphere of influence is expanding exponentially. I have complete access to kingdom things, and this is my season of prosperity.

Exhale

What is your prayer for today? What is God saying to you?

_____

_____

_____

_____

_____

Day 15

I TAKE CARE OF BUSINESS

Let all things be done decently and in order.
—1 Corinthians 14:40

Inhale

All my business dealings are carried out with godly character and integrity. I follow through in all aspects of life and business, carrying all visions and projects to completion.

Exhale

What is your prayer for today? What is God saying to you?

_____

_____

_____

_____

_____

_____

Day 16

I DO GOD'S WILL

Go therefore and make disciples of all the nations, baptizing them in the name of the Father and of the Son and of the Holy Spirit.
—Matthew 28:19

Inhale

I can and will do all God wants me to do in ministry. He has fully empowered me to carry to fruition His plans to spread the Gospel throughout all the earth.

Exhale

What is your prayer for today? What is God saying to you?

_____

_____

_____

_____

_____

Day 17

I AM MORE THAN A CONQUEROR

Yet in all these things we are more than conquerors through Him who loved us.
—Romans 8:37

INHALE

I am more than a conqueror who stands in the victory of Jesus. I declare, in Him, I am above the influence and plans of the enemy.

EXHALE

What is your prayer for today? What is God saying to you?

_____

_____

_____

_____

_____

_____

Day 18

I PROSPER IN ALL THINGS

Beloved, I pray that you may prosper in all things and be in health, just as your soul prospers.
—3 John 1:2

Inhale

I am healthy, physically fit, spiritually, emotionally, and intellectually equipped.

Exhale

What is your prayer for today? What is God saying to you?

_____

_____

_____

_____

_____

_____

Eikonic Leadership

Day 19

I LEAD A BLESSED GENERATION

Blessed is the man who fears the Lord, who delights greatly in His commandments. His descendants will be mighty on earth; the generation of the upright will be blessed.
—Psalm 112:1–2

Inhale

I declare a legacy of faith over my life. I will store up blessings for future generations. My life is marked by excellence and integrity. Because I make right choices and take steps in faith, others want to follow me. God's abundance is surrounding my life today.

Exhale

What is your prayer for today? What is God saying to you?

_____

_____

_____

_____

Eikonic Leadership

Day 20

I AM ACCELERATED

"Yes indeed, it won't be long now." God's Decree. "Things are going to happen so fast your head will swim, one thing fast on the heels of the other. You won't be able to keep up. Everything will be happening at once—and everywhere you look, blessings! Blessings like wine pouring off the mountains and hills. I'll make everything right again for my people Israel.
—Amos 9:13–14, the Message

Inhale

God will accelerate His plan for my life as I put my trust in Him. In Him, I will accomplish my dreams faster than I thought possible. He has blessings that will thrust me years ahead.

Exhale

What is your prayer for today? What is God saying to you?

_____

_____

_____

Day 21

I AM ALIVE IN CHRIST

I have been crucified with Christ; it is no longer I who live, but Christ lives in me; and the life which I now live in the flesh I live by faith in the Son of God, who loved me and gave Himself for me.
—Galatians 2:20

Inhale

I decree today I am dead to myself. I am made alive only in You, Father God. I command everything I say and do to line up with that truth, in the name of Jesus.

Exhale

What is your prayer for today? What is God saying to you?

_____

_____

_____

_____

Day 22

I AM SPIRIT-LED

Pursue peace with all people, and holiness, without which no one will see the Lord: looking carefully lest anyone fall short of the grace of God; lest any root of bitterness springing up cause trouble, and by this many become defiled.
—Hebrews 12:14–15

Inhale

I do not get offended nor am I led by my emotions. I'm dead to that. Rather, I'm led by the Spirit.

Exhale

What is your prayer for today? What is God saying to you?

_____

_____

_____

_____

_____

Day 23

I WILL NOT BE SILENCED

*For God has not given us a spirit of fear, but
of power and of love and of a sound mind.*
—2 Timothy 1:7

Inhale

I will speak out in boldness of the goodness of my Savior to all those I encounter. I will not be silenced.

Exhale

What is your prayer for today? What is God saying to you?

_____

_____

_____

_____

_____

_____

Eikonic Leadership

Day 24

I HAVE A VICTOR'S MIND-SET

For whatever is born of God overcomes the world. And this is the victory that has overcome the world—our faith.
—1 John 5:4

Inhale

God has made me an overcomer. I do not feel sorry for myself nor allow my past nor current circumstances to define me. I have a victor's mindset.

Exhale

What is your prayer for today? What is God saying to you?

_____

_____

_____

_____

EIKONIC LEADERSHIP

Day 25

I AM SURROUNDED BY THE RIGHT PEOPLE

*As iron sharpens iron, so a man sharpens
the countenance of his friend.*
—Proverbs 27:17

Inhale

This is a season of favor and increase for, around and through me. I am connecting with right people and networks that align with my purpose and bring forth destiny. I am connecting with people who speak life to me and who are not afraid to challenge me beyond mediocracy and into excellence in all areas.

Exhale

What is your prayer for today? What is God saying to you?

_____

_____

_____

_____

Day 26

I HAVE MORE THAN I CAN ASK

Now to Him who is able to do exceedingly abundantly above all that we ask or think, according to the power that works in us.
—Ephesians 3:20

Inhale

It is my season of more than enough, my season of supernatural finances and debt freedom. God will do even more than I imagine, transitioning and positioning me on a path toward promotion—spiritually, physically, emotionally, financially, and relationally.

Exhale

What is your prayer for today? What is God saying to you?

Day 27

I AM A SURVIVOR

Behold, I give you the authority to trample on serpents and scorpions, and over all the power of the enemy, and nothing shall by any means hurt you.
—Luke 10:19

Inhale

I will survive the enemy's plots, stop signs, explosives, booby traps, and negative words against me and my loved ones. At all times, I will sound the alarm and shout hallelujah!

Exhale

What is your prayer for today? What is God saying to you?

_____

_____

_____

_____

_____

Day 28

GOD DOES GREAT THINGS FOR ME

*The LORD has done great things
for us, and we are glad.*
—Psalm 126:3

INHALE

God is doing more great things for me. He is preparing a table before me in the presence of my enemies that I receive now in the name of Jesus.

EXHALE

What is your prayer for today? What is God saying to you?

Eikonic Leadership

Day 29

I AM CHOSEN

But you are a chosen generation, a royal priesthood, a holy nation, His own special people, that you may proclaim the praises of Him who called you out of darkness into His marvelous light.
—2 PETER 2:9

INHALE

I am uniquely gifted to influence and impact a group, nation, and generation. I will move them beyond the status quo, from the average into the exceptional. I empower them to believe the vision is not only possible, but it also is achievable.

EXHALE

What is your prayer for today? What is God saying to you?

_____

_____

_____

_____

Day 30

I AM OVERTAKEN BY BLESSINGS

*And all these blessings shall come upon you and overtake you, because you obey the voice of the L*ORD *your God.*
—DEUTERONOMY 28:2

INHALE

I declare opportunities will chase me from this day forward. I know and believe my God will supply all of my needs according to His riches in glory. I speak this into the atmosphere and receive it.

EXHALE

What is your prayer for today? What is God saying to you?

_____

_____

_____

_____

Eikonic Leadership

Day 31

I SUBMIT TO THE TIMING OF GOD

...of the sons of Issachar who had understanding of the times, to know what Israel ought to do.
—1 Chronicles 12:32

Inhale

I declare and decree I understand the times and seasons. I know what to do. I submit to the timing of the Lord's favor in my life, and I obey Him.

Exhale

What is your prayer for today? What is God saying to you?

_____

_____

_____

_____

_____

Eikonic Leadership

NOTES

INTRODUCTION
YOU ARE EIKONIC

1. Merriam-Websters.com, s.v. "iconic," https://www.merriam-webster.com/dictionary/iconic.
2. Ibid.
3. Ibid.
4. Kendra Cherry, "What Is Laissez-Faire Leadership?" VeryWellMind.com, October 23, 2018, https://www.verywellmind.com/what-is-laissez-faire-leadership-2795316.
5. Kendra Cherry, "Autocratic Leadership," VeryWellMind.com, October 22, 2018, https://www.verywellmind.com/what-is-autocratic-leadership-2795314.
6. What Is Democratic/Participative Leadership? How Collaboration Can Boost Morale?" St. Thomas University Online, June 1, 2019, https://online.stu.edu/articles/education/democratic-participative-leadership.aspx.

Chapter 1
The Eikonic Leader Profile

1. *The Breakfast Club*, written, directed, and produced by John Hughes (1985; Universal City, CA: Universal Pictures).
2. *Pretty in Pink,* directed by Howard Deutch, written by John Hughes (1986; Hollywood, CA: Paramount Pictures).
3. Zoie O'Brien, "Queen Thought Diana Was a Misfit but Now She 'Radiates Out of William and Harry,'" Express.co.uk, March 7, 2016, www.express.co.uk/news/royal/650438/Queen-Diana-William-Harry-Prince-William-Prince-Harry-Queen-Elizabeth.
4. CliftonStrengths, s.v. "ideation," https://www.gallupstrengthscenter.com/cms/en-us/gmj/679/ideation.
5. Ibid.
6. Oxford Living Dictionaries, s.v. "passion," https://en.oxforddictionaries.com/definition/passion.
7. Merriam-Webster.com, s.v. "vision," https://www.merriam-webster.com/dictionary/vision.
8. Oxford Living Dictionaries, s.v. "discipline," https://en.oxforddictionaries.com/definition/discipline.
9. Dictionary.com, s.v. "discipline," https://www.dictionary.com/browse/discipline.
10. Merriam-Websters.com, s.v. "risk-taking," https://www.merriam-webster.com/dictionary/risk-taking.
11. Oxford Living Dictionaries, s.v. "excellence," https://en.oxforddictionaries.com/definition/excellence.

12. Merriam-Websters.com, s.v. "mediocre," https://www.merriam-webster.com/dictionary/mediocre.

13. Ibid.

CHAPTER 2
NINE SPIRITS THAT BREAK THE EIKONIC LEADER—AND HOW TO BEAT THEM

1. Jennifer LeClaire, "What the Spirit of Python Really Wants," CharismaMag.com, September 25, 2014, https://www.charismamag.com/blogs/the-plumb-line/21396-what-the-python-spirit-really-wants.

2. Merriam-Websters.com, s.v. "assassinate," https://www.merriam-webster.com/dictionary/assassinate.

3. James C. McKinley and Robbie Brown, "Sex Scandal Threatens a Georgia Pastor's Empire," *New York Times*, September 25, 2010.

4. "America's Ghandi: Rev. Martin Luther King Jr.," *Time*, January 3, 1964, http://content.time.com/time/subscriber/article/0,33009,940759-3,00.html.

5. Lucy Duncan, "Creative Maladjustment: A Prayer in Honor of Dr. Martin Luther King, Jr.," Acting in Faith Blog, April 4, 2012, https://www.afsc.org/friends/creative-maladjustment-prayer-honor-martin-luther-king-jr.

6. Leonardo Blair, "Pastor Andrew Stoecklein Was Inside Church When He Attempted Suicide, Police Reveal," *The Christian Post*, August 29, 2018, https://www.christianpost.com/news/pastor-andrew-stoecklein-was-inside-church-when-he-attempted-suicide-police-reveal.html.

7. Thom Rainer, "5 Reasons Pastors Get Depressed (and Why They Don't Talk About It)," Southern Equip, htttp+//eau.ip.slots.edu/article/5-reasons-pastors-get-depressed-dont-talk/.

Chapter 3
An Unconventional Individual

1. "The 5 Love Languages Defined," 5LoveLanguages.com, https://www.5lovelanguages.com/2018/06/the-five-love-languages-defined/.

Chapter 4
Building Your Eikonic Circle of Trust—Your Tribe

1. Colin Haig Jr., Facebook.com, N.d.
2. John Gray, "Gethsemane: Rockets Don't Have Reverse," Reno Walker Ministries, December 22, 2017, https://www.youtube.com/watch?v=TzyQ8y0cJeY&feature=youtu.be.

Chapter 5
Church, Can You Handle Me?

1. PreceptAustin.org, "Apostle-Apostolos (Greek Word Study)," https://www.preceptaustin.org/apostle_-_apostolos.
2. Merriam-Webster.com, s.v. "alignment," https://www.merriam-webster.com/dictionary/alignment.

3. Ryan LeStrange, "#AlignmentIsKey," https://www.facebook.com/RyanLeStrangePage/photos/a.504114842936154/1778906038790355/?type=3&theater.

CHAPTER 6
ANOINTED BUT UNANNOUNCED

1. Gray, "Gethsemane: Rockets Don't Have Reverse."
2. Ryan LeStrange, Facebook.com, December 25, 2017, https://www.facebook.com/RyanLeStrangePage/posts/there-is-a-reckless-remnant-that-will-rise-out-of-the-glory-of-god-their-trainin/2235176019830019/.
3. Lance Wallnau, "How the '7 Mountains' Will Be 'Taken' by Individuals Like You," 1 Kingdom for All, December 10, 2014, https://www.youtube.com/watch?v=bhRwr7p_8M8.
4. Ibid.
5. Ibid.

CHAPTER 7
YOUR SECRET'S OUT

1. "Positive Daily Affirmations: Is There Science Behind It?" Positive Psychology Program, March 5, 2019, https://positivepsychologyprogram.com/daily-affirmations/#positive-affirmations
2. Ibid.
3. Ibid.
4. Joel Osteen, *The Power of I Am* (Nashville, TN: FaithWords, 2016).

5. Oxford Living Dictionaries, s.v. "boundary," https://en.oxforddictionaries.com/definition/boundary.

6. "Dr. Henry Cloud: Leading with Boundaries," CBN.com, http://www1.cbn.com/700club/dr-henry-cloud-leading-boundaries.

7. Dr. Matthew L. Stevenson III, "5 Signs of Healthy Loyalty," Facebook.com, February 22, 2018, https://m.facebook.com/story.php?story_fbid=1670934949639567&id=489060771160330.

8. LaBryant Friend, "You are not really a loyalist…" Facebook.com, August 26, 2016, https://m.facebook.com/story.php?story_fbid=10100303812549802&id=79103408.

ADDITIONAL RESOURCES

Throughout the book, I named several books and leadership resources that have been invaluable to me on my journey as an iconic leader as well as in my service of mentoring other leaders. Here is the full list, plus a few more. I hope you find it helpful.

Baron, Renee and Elizabeth Wagele. *The Enneagram Made Easy.* New York: HarperOne, 1994.

Chand, Samuel. *Leadership Pain.* Nashville, TN: Thomas Nelson, 2015.

Chestnut, PhD, Beatrice. *The 9 Types of Leadership.* New York: Post Hill Press, 2017.

Cloud, Henry. *Boundaries for Leaders.* New York: Harper Business, 2013.

Copeland, Germaine. *Prayers That Avail Much.* Shippensburg, PA: Harrison House, 2005.

Covey, Steven. *The 7 Habits of Highly Successful People.* New York: Simon and Schuster, 1989.

Cron, Ian Morgan and Suzanne Stabile. *The Road Back to You.* Westmont, IL: InterVarsity Press, 2016.

Maxwell, John and Les Parrott, PhD. *25 Ways to Win with People.* New York: HarperCollins Leadership, 2005.

Maxwell, John. *Becoming a Person of Influence.* New York: HarperCollins Leadership, 2006.

———. *The 5 Levels of Leadership.* Nashville, TN: CenterStreet, 2013.

Morin, Amy. *13 Things Mentally Strong People Don't Do.* New York: William Morrow, 2017.

Osteen, Joel. *The Power of I Am.* Nashville, TN: FaithWords, 2016.

Scazzero, Geri with Peter Scazzero. *I Quit.* Grand Rapids, MI: Zondervan, 2010.

Tom Rath. *StrengthsFinder 2.0.* New York: Gallup Press, 2007.

ABOUT THE AUTHOR

Ansonya Burke is a powerful instrument God is using to reach people where they are. She has a charming and humble personality. She is a leader of leaders, teacher, coach, mentor, and consultant with a no-nonsense approach to ministry and leadership. She uses her God-given gifts to encourage others to seek a personal, minute-by-minute relationship with their Lord and Savior. Ansonya believes leaders should be both committed to excellence as well as possess the spirit of excellence. She believes Jehovah-Jireh, our provider, deserves our very best efforts.

Well-known for stretching believers to the limit of their abilities, she is called to impart and activate gifts and raise up strong leaders in the body of Christ. Her desire is to impact the world by restoring, perfecting, building, and training believers to fulfill their destiny through serving their leadership through excellence in their churches and corporate settings. Ansonya aspires to encourage and impart biblically based principles in leaders to advance the kingdom of God. She develops and mentors their five-fold ministry gifts and talents and helps them to establish a committed pursuit of destiny and purpose.

Ansonya has an apostolic anointing that reaches into the depths of her being to draw on her knowledge, experience, and wisdom, and pour out unselfishly into the lives of others. Ansonya's heart's desire is for ministry and business leaders to experience God personally and know Him in a powerful way so that they may enter and lead others into His gates.

With a heart for leadership, Ansonya's vision is teach others to utilize AIR—activating, imparting, and releasing—to birth successful personal, professional, and spiritual relationships. Her goal is to encourage, equip, and support leaders to effectively reach, disciple, and multiply healthy Christian leaders in ministry, mentorship, and the corporate marketplace.

Ansonya is the mother of two children—Master Quentin and Princess Aniyah Burke. A graduate of the University of Arizona with a bachelor's degree in family studies and counseling, she holds a master's degree in organizational management from the University of Phoenix. She currently works in the corporate marketplace as a manager, leader, and mentor.

Saved since her early tender years, Ansonya accepted her calling and submitted her life to ministry in May 2002. She was ordained as an evangelist and minister in December 2004 and has served under many Christian leaders as confidant and assistant to the pastor and first lady, praise and worship leader, choir director, executive secretary, finance ministry, teacher, accountability partner, conference coordinator and speaker, spiritual and professional mentor, and inspirational speaker. Three places she is inspired to reach people of God—churches, conferences, and in the corporate arenas.

www.ingramcontent.com/pod-product-compliance
Lightning Source LLC
Chambersburg PA
CBHW031241290426
44109CB00012B/382